The Evolution of the Law Firm Library Function:
Transformation and integration into the business of law

EDITED BY FRANCESCA RAMADAN

Commissioning editor
Alex Davies

Editorial assistant
Francesca Ramadan

Published by
Globe Law and Business Ltd
3 Mylor Close
Horsell
Woking
Surrey GU21 4DD
United Kingdom
Tel: +44 20 3745 4770
www.globelawandbusiness.com

ISBN: 978-1-78358-340-9
A catalogue record for this book is available from the British Library

Contents

Contents

Executive summary

It is undeniable that the modern legal library is caught in a transformative stage. The aftereffects of the 2008 financial crisis continue to ripple through the legal profession in general; although global economies are in recovery, progress is slow and incremental, and support functions are at the forefront of the agenda as firms look to cut operational costs. Often seen by firm management as unnecessary and outdated, legal libraries are facing a double-pronged challenge: it is now essential for librarians to demonstrate the continuing value of their profession whilst battling with shrinking budgets and the development of new, disruptive technologies that are transforming working practices and processes at a rapid rate. This has meant that now, more than ever, libraries are at risk.

However, the traditional knee-jerk responses to such threats and challenges – such as downsizing and outsourcing – are now not enough. Instead, the modern librarian has been compelled to innovate, transforming their role to one that embraces the possibilities that new digital resources bring and which has become more centered on information management. Similarly, the way in which the library functions has been forced to change in response to economic pressures; like other firm departments, the law library increasingly must apply principles and practices from the corporate world to its operations, in order to reduce costs and improve services. Indeed, the role of the library is transforming in the face of a dynamic and sometimes hostile climate, reforming itself from a semi-autonomous department to a fully integrated and agile facility that must embed itself solidly in a firm's everyday activities and respond quickly and efficiently to its challenges and queries.

In this period of extreme upheaval, it is essential for both library and firm management to seek the right guidance in negotiating these challenges. Heavy emphasis is often placed on technological innovation and digital resources, and their current and future impact, due to the exciting and revolutionary potential these modernizations bring. However, what is of more value is tackling those difficult issues libraries face as they reform their operations to more resemble a corporate model and as the focus shifts towards profitability. Packed with constructive advice and fascinating insight from a range of industry experts – from librarians to knowledge officers and consultants – *The Evolution of the Law Firm Library Function: Transformation and integration into the business of law* seeks to provide the most pertinent and practical intelligence about the current challenges and the most effective ways of negotiating them. Invaluable advice is supplemented by pioneering, real-world examples of alternative methods of library management that can provide a solid foundation for application and implementation.

The concept of the modern law library goes hand-in-hand with running your library like a business, which requires being fiscally responsible, utilizing metrics to measure ROI and value, and ensuring your target audience is knowledgeable of and satisfied with the solutions and services the library provides. The difficulty for most librarians and library management, however, is taking those first steps. In chapter 1, Monice Kaczorowski – principal of AGOG Consulting – provides guidance in understanding the various tools that support the running of a library like a business. The multiple ways metrics can be utilized – from monitoring usage and trends to adjusting a library's portfolio of products and contents – are discussed, before various metrics are offered as a starting point for implementation.

In the current economy and competitive marketplace, law firms have dramatically changed the way they conduct business. The impact of these developments has rippled throughout all departments; however, nowhere has it been felt more acutely than in the law library. Library staff have been tasked to wear multiple hats and take on more responsibility, whilst simultaneously being expected to do more with less. There is growing pressure to meet new demands or face being rendered redundant. In chapter 2, Kara Buzga and Tunisia Johnson – paralegal manager and legal information administrator at Mayer Brown LLP, respectively – make the case that it is the library's ability to collaborate that will guarantee its future. Employing their knowledge and expertise, they offer guidance to those who want to move from siloed working practices to a more synergic approach in order to continue delivering excellent service to both internal and external clients.

In these times of change, it is essential to revolutionize the library's ways of working; however, it is not always easy to be the pioneer. Difficult choices and unanticipated challenges are all part of the processes of transformation and innovation. To gain insight into potential pitfalls would be invaluable for many looking to trigger the evolution of their own library department; however, this kind of intelligence is not always readily available. Fortunately, in chapter 3, Patrick DiDomenico – chief knowledge officer at Ogletree Deakins – supplies an exclusive insight into the absorption of his firm's library functions into the knowledge management department, addressing the impetus for the change, its execution, what went well, and what went wrong.

It is well established that research is essential to the daily operations of a large law firm. With the right answer sets, firms can build business with new clients and serve existing clients efficiently, increasing revenue. Thousands of questions and answers fly across a large law firm like a daily network of data and unstructured knowledge, seeking organization and application. In chapter 4, Scott D Bailey – global director of research services at Squire Patton Boggs – and David Kamien – CEO of Mind-Alliance Systems – propose that, with the right people, processes, and tools, law firm libraries can move from learning about the firm in a supporting role to preparing and leading actionable business processes in advance. Partnering with the multiple practice relationships and business development leaders to act on these insights will affix the law firm library in a permanent and valued place in the law firm business model of tomorrow.

There is a general consensus that law students, upon graduation, are not prepared to engage in the modern practice of law. This encompasses both students' technological preparedness as well as understanding of the business of legal practice. Lack of exposure to these concepts during law school can lead to a delay in meaningful contributions by new associates and fed-up clients. The response to this problem – or even acknowledging it as a problem at all – has varied widely between and within law schools. In addition to reviewing some of the general trends and individual approaches taken by law schools around the country, chapter 5 by Jocelyn K Sagherian – reference librarian at the Fordham Law School Library – discusses ways law in which firm librarians can assist in this new approach to legal education with the ultimate goal of improving the bottom line of the law firm.

For international law firms, with operations around the world, law libraries have arguably run at a 24/7 pace for at least a decade. But even mid-size law libraries now see attorneys tapping research and making requests around-the-clock. A mix of technology and collaboration – both inside and outside the library – offers a path forward. What's the right formula for meeting an increasingly complex mix of requests? What are law librarians doing now to keep up, and what thoughts and advice do firms have for librarians still coming to grips with how to truly be open around the clock? In chapter 6, Jim Haggerty – vice president of LAC Group – utilizes his expertise in providing solutions to achieve unparalleled research and competitive intelligence to offer the potential answer to these pressing questions.

In chapter 7, Cynthia Brown – director of research services, Littler Mendelson PC – and Jill L Kilgore – research librarian, Littler Mendelson PC – explore how a client problem found its solution in a library. In a novel business development approach – which ultimately helped capture the work of in-house counsel – the library drew on established information-gathering capabilities to provide data visualizations and enhance attorney services. The application of these data analytics helped identify inefficiencies in a client's human resource functions and the implementation of solutions. The case study in this chapter highlights these hidden opportunities made possible by established library practices, and offers insight on how to gain access to potential new projects through interdepartmental leadership.

With the cost of office space increasing in most cities, the biggest financial burden on any law firm is the cost of their premises. Business teams are being squeezed for space; this often has an impact on libraries, which usually have the largest footprint of any of these teams. In chapter 8, CJ Anderson – head of information and research at Linklaters LLP, London – outlines the topics those starting to make the change from physical to mobile need to consider by using the evolution of Linklaters' information and research service. This serves to illustrate the factors that have changed the physical library and the impact these have had on CJ's team – affecting the resources that they buy and the services they provide, their relationship with the IT teams, and the behavioral changes of the lawyers they support.

In the years ahead, software will perform legal tasks previously reserved for lawyers, paralegals, and information professionals; a great deal of the money paid by clients for those legal services will go to the architects of that software. Will this be an information oligopoly, or will the benefits be widespread? In the final chapter, Ed Walters and Sean Tate – CEO and AI sandbox product manager at Fastcase Inc., respectively – make the case that the answer to this question, in part, lies with how broadly the providers of legal services and information participate in artificial intelligence. Guidance will be offered for those information and legal professionals looking to reap the gains of the new economy and harness the potential that the broad-based renaissance in legal services brings.

About the authors

CJ Anderson is head of information and research (I&R) at Linklaters LLP in London. She qualified as a librarian in 1996 and worked as an information professional in a number of sectors (public, civil service, and pharmaceutical) before joining Linklaters in 2001 as an information advisor in a practice and then leading I&R for a global division. In her current position, CJ has developed and led a truly global team, working across offices on a regular basis. CJ became a chartered member of CILIP in 2000 and is a passionate advocate for the professional development of Linklaters' I&R teams. She believes in working smarter, not harder, with a focus on self-service desktop products and exploiting overlaps with other teams to provide streamlined information and research solutions.

Scott D Bailey is the global director of research services at Squire Patton Boggs, managing the complex international KM and R&D needs of a law firm with 46 offices in 21 countries. With thousands of internal and external clients in a top 10 "most global" firm, his team of researchers is approachable, energetic, and engaging whilst delivering a high level of experienced analysis. He recently co-authored an article for the March/April issue of the *FinTech Law Report*, entitled "Use of artificial intelligence for smart contracts and blockchains". As a champion of success through authentic intelligence and building knowledge community, Scott works collaboratively with a variety of professionals beyond the legal industry; he believes in creativity and fostering situations where gathering up the right people and getting everyone going in the same direction leads to multiplied benefits for all stakeholders.

Cynthia Brown is the director of research services at Littler Mendelson, the world's largest employment and labor law practice representing management, where she has bridged the worlds of the library and knowledge management since 2007. Her previous experience includes working as in-house counsel for four years at a small risk management firm, as an account manager and training consultant at LexisNexis, and running a solo library in Salt Lake City at Jones Waldo Holbrook & McDonough.

Kara Buzga has served as a paralegal manager for over two decades, with management experience on both the plaintiff and defense side. Among her experiences on the plaintiff's side, she successfully organized, managed, and implemented a document retention policy team and maintained various firm-wide litigation holds while upholding preservation requirements. Currently on the defense side, her experience includes case needs assessments and strategic management of workflow and work assignments. Her role is to be a source of innovation, intelligence, and change. Kara collaborates with matter responsible lawyers and senior associates from all practice groups, on a matter-by-matter basis, to implement matter management tools and techniques in order to ensure that matters are executed efficiently and within budget. Kara is also responsible for increasing and maximizing the utilization, efficiency, and effectiveness of her firm's paralegals.

Patrick DiDomenico is the chief knowledge officer for Ogletree, Deakins, Nash, Smoak & Stewart, PC, an international labor and employment law firm with approximately 900 attorneys in 52 offices. Patrick also serves on the firm's Technology Strategy Committee, Research and Development Council, and Innovation Summit Committee. Before his knowledge management career, he was a practicing litigation attorney for more than eight years. He is also the author of *Knowledge Management for Lawyers* (2015), published by the American Bar Association, and publishes the LawyerKM blog (www.LawyerKM.com) in his spare time. He is a Fellow in the College of Law Practice Management, a frequent speaker on KM, legal technology and legal innovation topics, and an advisor to legal technology startups.

Jim Haggerty has 21 years of experience with the legal industry and information services. He joined LAC Group, a provider of information and knowledge management solutions, from LexisNexis, where he was vice president for the Am Law 100 and large corporate legal departments. At LAC Group, Haggerty oversees the expansion of the company's offerings for on-site and virtual librarians at law firms, corporations and any organization wanting unparalleled research and competitive intelligence. Haggerty received his bachelor's degree from the State University of New York.

Tunisia Johnson is a legal information administrator at Mayer Brown LLP, New York office. She has worked in the library field for 20 years in a variety of roles, ranging from library filer to library assistant. Later in her career she returned to education to receive her MLS degree; upon her completion of the program, she was then promoted to her current position, in which she manages the library department. Tunisia is responsible for paring down duplicate print materials, focusing on digital content, organizing training programs by vendors for specific practice areas, negotiating vendor contracts, and providing legal research assistance. These tasks require her collaboration with several departments within the firm and across other offices. Tunisia is very knowledgeable of the many legal research resources available, with her skills and expertise earning the respect of her firm's attorneys and paralegals, alongside her library colleagues in various offices.

Monice M Kaczorowski, MLS is principal of AGOG Consulting, where she leads client engagements and develops resources that are focused on process improvement and library modernization. In collaboration with her client, Feit Consulting, she recently co-authored their most recent white paper release, *Beyond Virtualization: Transforming The Law Library* – a comprehensive resource on the modern law library. As a former chief knowledge officer, she has been a proponent of law firm KM as a way to improve attorney workflow and foster efficiencies within the practice of law. Monice has a keen sense for the large picture while understanding the micro-nuances of legal information management.

David Kamien is the CEO of Mind-Alliance Systems (www.mind-alliance.com). Mind-Alliance provides law firms with solutions in areas including business development research, knowledge management, and innovation. He is also the product owner of the MindPeer research management software system (www.mindpeer.com). David has supported leading clients such as Squire Patton Boggs, Ogletree Deakins, Sidley Austin, Shearman & Sterling, NATO, the Rockefeller Foundation, the World Bank, the US Department of Homeland Security, Raytheon, and the Center for Strategic & International Studies. He is the editor of the seminal McGraw-Hill Homeland Security Handbook (2005, 2012 editions) and the inventor of a patented method for improving organizational information sharing and collaboration. David holds a law degree from the Academic College of Law and a BA from Hebrew University.

Jill L Kilgore is currently a research librarian at Littler Mendelson, PC. She received her MLS from Emporia State University. Prior to her career as a law librarian, she studied art history and studio art at the University of Kansas. Her areas of interest include emerging technologies, digital scholarship, visual resource management, and social justice.

Jocelyn K Sagherian works with the Maloney Law Library at the Fordham University School of Law, providing reference assistance to students and faculty. At Fordham, she has taught courses on legal practice technology and basic legal research, as well as classes on competitive intelligence, eDiscovery, and patent and trademark legal research. Prior to working with Fordham, Jocelyn was the manager of library services at Gardere Wynne Sewell LLP (now Foley Gardere). She also worked as an account executive and distance learning specialist with LexisNexis and as an associate at Schulte Roth & Zabel LLP. Jocelyn received her BA from the University of Florida, her JD/MPA from the George Washington University, and her MLS from the University of Buffalo.

Sean Tate is the AI Sandbox Product Manager at Fastcase, Inc, where he works to democratize the law by creating a read-write technological environment allowing for the truly unique analysis of legal data with artificial intelligence tools. Sean has been a member of the Fastcase team since 2014, working on projects such as daily automation of Statutes and Acts and Fastcase's TopForm bankruptcy filing software. Sean has a Bachelor of Arts from Ohio Wesleyan University.

Ed Walters is the CEO of Fastcase, a legal publishing company based in Washington DC. Before founding Fastcase, Ed worked at Covington & Burling, in Washington DC and Brussels, where his practice focused on corporate advisory work for software companies and sports leagues, and intellectual property litigation. Ed earned an AB from Georgetown University and a JD from the University of Chicago. He is an adjunct professor at the Georgetown University Law Center and at Cornell Tech, where he teaches The Law of Robots, a class about the frontiers of law and technology.

Chapter 1: The value of metrics in the modern library

By Monice Kaczorowski, principal of AGOG Consulting

The road to a modern law library is paved with metrics. A forward-thinking, business-oriented law librarian has a variety of metrics at hand and should be prepared to use them regularly to tell the story of fiscal responsibility, to substantiate the need for improvement, to demonstrate value, and to link them logically back to goals.

Some legal professionals may be surprised to learn that many law librarians administer budgets larger than those of most small businesses in the United States. According to Altman and Weil, library expense remains one of the top five budget items for a law firm. Being fiscally responsible is a necessity and providing management with critical information relative to when, where and why things are being purchased starts the ball rolling. Moving beyond the when, where and why is the point where metrics really begin to make the difference.

Change is the only constant; as such, the best law firms and their law libraries need to remain agile. Agility requires tools to respond to needs and make sound decisions. In the modern law library, these tools are often metrics. Law librarians have any number of current metrics available to them for capturing utilization and trends, providing concrete data for leveraging contracts or staffing negotiations, and allowing the library to adjust its portfolio of products and content as requirements change. Additionally, many more options have been developed to supplement the ones already available.

Forward-thinking librarians may consider combining current metrics with newly evolving metric tools and utilizing a more comprehensive arsenal of metrics to show how the library aligns itself to the firm's strategic plan and supports the firm's goals and objectives. There is more to metrics than easy-to-collect data. While providing useful information, isolated statistics only tell part of the library story. Moving beyond general reporting of metrics to analysis provides the librarian intel to demonstrate to the executive committee and managing partners just what targets are being hit or missed, what measures of performance need to be addressed and in what ways the library is currently contributing to, and can potentially contribute to, the firm's bottom line.

The various metric tools described below help provide an accurate measure of ROI and showcase the comprehensive value of content and services provided by the library.

Fiscal responsibility

Budget

A well-developed budget can serve as a metric tool in itself throughout the year. It defines the library's goals and can be utilized to measure progress. It allows one to measure whether funds are being spent as planned, and whether costs were accurately forecasted and budgeted. If the library is to be viewed as fiscally responsible and as gatekeeper of the firm's bottom line, analyzing spend and revenue to accommodate changing needs must be ongoing.

The library budget should be a clear reflection of the actual library revenue and expense. Included should be sub-budget lines that reflect the detail necessary to explain the total library operation. In working with finance, fine-tuned monthly reports should be helpful to both management and the library.

Continuously collecting data and preparing a budget to meet identified needs is the mark of a fiscally responsible business-oriented law librarian. Below are considerations when preparing a law library budget. Thorough budgeting leads to successful planning and operations. Asking questions and investigating potential financial impacts is critical to accurate budgeting:

- Does the budget reflect the organization's strategic initiatives?
- Are all revenue streams being captured and monitored?
- Are costs being accurately reflected?

Shaping, structuring and restructuring the law library budget, combining best past practices with newly identified solutions while aligning with the firm's anticipated needs each year, capitalizes on metrics and highlights the value of analysis of data. Optimizing the utilization of financial information – both expense and revenue – demonstrates the benefit of running the library as a business. As a business unit within the firm, the law library should be a necessary component in the firm's strategic plan. When a department is one of the top five budget items in an organization, budgets cannot be prepared in a vacuum nor should they be based solely upon the spending practices of the previous year. As annual budgets are prepared, the expense of resources and initiatives should be proactively evaluated to make sure they remain in actual alignment with firm-wide goals, trends and strategic initiatives.

Billing invoices and cost recovery

Law firm administrators and librarians continually struggle to justify expense of online resources. As clients continue to push back on online charges, LEXIS and WESTLAW have provided electronic tools that provide librarians access to real time data for assessing usage and cost recovery. Tools such as Power Invoice and Quickview, while mainly used for billing, can be analyzed more deeply to determine the need for more education or different types of education would benefit users. Additionally, reviewing costs and usage sheds lights on the value of content by vendor and is beneficial in negotiating new contracts. Collaboration between library and finance can produce valuable monthly billing reports for cost recovery.

Demonstrating value

Statistics

To better measure and justify a library's value, librarians may elect to collect and analyze statistics that reflect tasks completed by staff. Compiling research statistics by type of question, practice group and patron provides intel for identifying heavy users of library services. Those heavy users can be rallied and solicited as library champions when support is needed to get budgets passed, purchase new products, and further new initiatives. These same statistics can be compiled and presented to firm administrators to demonstrate how specific practice groups utilize library services.

The compilation of metrics from external and internal resources provides a valuable foundation of information necessary to provide accurate substantiation of ROI to management. The development of procedures and discovery of technology will streamline the tasks necessary to compile metrics from external and internal resources and will ultimately provide for an easier and less time-consuming process. Consider the following list of data points:

- ERM utilization reports;
- Portal user statistics;
- Practice group resource allocation;
- Budget analysis;
- Check-in/routing/processing of invoices; and
- E-billing/cost recovery.

Billable hours

Not all law libraries bill for research services; however, billing for library time is a powerful metric and a pillar of firm revenue. Using monthly billing reports that can be obtained through the firm finance group provides additional valuable metrics. Analyzing monthly data can be utilized to determine which attorneys are billing library time and which are not, providing valuable information to firm management. The collaboration between finance, practice group leaders and the library can result in the establishment of billing guidelines, the creation of consistent research descriptions and titles that attorneys want to appear on billing statements, and will open discussions around what can and cannot be billed to clients. Anticipating what will generally be written off or considered overhead is valuable information during budget planning time and is important information during analysis. Additionally, these monthly billing reports can be used as metrics and can serve as a starting point for conversations with attorneys to explain the value of library services. Perhaps most importantly, these metrics allow the librarian new possibilities for recouping billable hours, proving ROI of staffing and salaries.

Such statistics not only illustrate the value of what the library does but can be used to justify non-billing positions. These positions are often misunderstood and yet are integral to supporting the library infrastructure. Statistics can also be used in annual reporting to management or in marketing the services and solutions of the library.

Need for improvement

ERM reports

As publishers move away from print to electronic resource delivery, the costs of publications and negotiated seat licenses continue to escalate. For the most part, publishers of electronic subscriptions include few metrics to measure usage. As a result, ERMs (electronic resource management) tools are fast becoming the essential resource for gathering library metrics. Furthermore, the potential data analysis and insight derived from an ERM, relative to evaluating electronic subscriptions for renewal or cancellation, may in fact help to offset the actual purchase price of the ERM.

Utilizing ERMs to actively monitor practice group resources and changing content can prove to be another valuable go-to metric tool for collection management. The reporting capabilities are useful in annual budget preparation. Being able to demonstrate infrequent usage to an attorney who insists the inability to live without a resource may be the necessary data used to support the eventual cancellation of infrequently used and costly items.

In terms of contract negotiations for electronic subscriptions, ERMs provide raw data regarding actual usage of online vendors. This is powerful information and can help guide decisions on retaining or canceling expensive subscriptions. It may also serve as leverage for negotiating lower fees if usage is low.

ERMs have morphed beyond just monitoring electronic subscriptions. They are multifunctional in support. They are capable of tracking reference requests, managing contract renewals, aiding client matter validation, and password management. ERMs are a robust tool with a myriad of capabilities for capturing metrics by:

- Identifying top users of online resources to inform them of database enhancements and additional training;
- Analyzing usage, allowing the library to market any under-utilized online resources;
- Tracking research and reference queries with online submission of research requests, providing a centralized place to manage library research requests and allowing for easy reporting of statistics;
- Tracking metrics making it easier to communicate the value of the library to firm management; and
- Avoiding out-of-contract costs by including warning screens and messaging in online databases to direct users to alternate resources when they go to excluded content.

ERMs provide client/matter number validation, allowing the library the capability to track and bill clients for time spent performing research on databases. Since many libraries are no longer a physical space, an ERM can support mobile research with access to online resources and passwords.

The key players in this space are TRG Group (Research Monitor), OneLog, and Lucidea (LookUp Precision). As described above, the ERM product suite is robust. Not all modules are initially necessary. Reassessment after implementation is advisable to determine the value of the metrics derived. Educating firm leadership and promoting the value of information gathered from a current ERM will make future ERM module purchases easier for management to justify as they will – with the help of the librarian – have already seen the power of the metrics derived by this tool.

User feedback

Another real-time metric often overlooked in the library is user feedback. Since the library provides a myriad of services, soliciting user feedback is valuable in determining what is and isn't working. User feedback is a vital component in the library's annual report to management and should be used to substantiate the value-added services and staff by presenting statistics and testimonials. Methods of user feedback to consider include:

- Conducting surveys to gather input from particular practice groups or the entire firm;
- A simple "how are we doing" at the end of every fulfilled library request;
- Holding focus groups for new initiatives; and
- One-on-one interviews with users to gather input on a certain topic, product or content use.

User feedback is a metric that allows for agile and timely course correction.

Association surveys

Library association annual or biannual salary surveys provide valuable metrics regarding salary, staffing patterns and librarian-attorney ratios, allowing for benchmarking libraries against peer firms. These surveys are an excellent resource for evaluating staffing and salaries at a firm against the market. Understanding the number of librarians to attorneys at peer firms and salary metrics are important and should be continually analyzed. If new services and support is to become a goal of the Law Library, staffing and salaries should be appropriately matched.

Storyboarding

Once the facts have been gathered and analyzed, consider creating a storyboard with your data and producing a visually rich presentation. Storyboarding is a powerful tool when the right charts and graphs are chosen in support of the key performance indicators (KPI) of the library. Branding library data using firm colors and logos further signifies alignment with the firm. Consider moving to a dashboard environment where this data is continually updated and becomes real-time. This not only provides you with a clear consolidated view, but it is a tool that demonstrates to firm administrators that the library is a keeper of even more valuable information and is an integrated player on the firm-wide team. The dashboard will also provide information that will allow the librarian and firm decision makers the ability to spot trends and drill down into a wealth of information over set periods of time. These dashboards can be built so that they align organizational data with organizational strategy. Many tools described earlier have dashboard capabilities.

Conclusion

Metrics provide the data necessary to confirm efficiency, prove fiscal responsibility, exhibit cost savings and identify increased profits. Metrics help to paint the picture of how specific library services support or improve firm practice and departmental initiatives. The decision around which metrics to call upon or refence should always include considerations of the stakeholders and what they need or would want to know. Metrics allow for analysis of trends, alerting the librarian to what services and support they should consider. The modern library is agile, utilizing metrics as an important tool in running the library like a business.

In an ever-changing environment in which the law library must constantly justify its existence, a regular reliance upon metrics is critical. Law librarians have an array of existing metrics to call upon, re-evaluate and analyze in the generation of reports and in the justification of costs. When the existing metrics are added to newly evolving metric tools, the ability to tell the story of fiscal responsibility, to substantiate the need for improvement and to demonstrate value becomes even more valuable and provides for the possibility of a real-time, visually compelling story – a story in which one of the top five budget items in a law firm is part of the solution, not part of the problem.

Chapter 2: Collaboration and coordination – the integration of the library into the "business of law"

By Kara Buzga, paralegal manager at Mayer Brown LLP, and Tunisia Johnson, legal information administrator at Mayer Brown LLP

In this new economy and competitive marketplace, law firms have dramatically changed the way they conduct business. Part of this change is due to increased globalization of law firms and their clients. Technological innovations designed to provide more streamlined services are a contributing factor; change can also be dictated by our clients. Librarians have been tasked to wear multiple hats and take on more responsibility; it is expected that we do more with less. We are working in fast-paced environments where our roles are being constantly evaluated, tried out and groomed. Inability to meet these new demands will eventually lead to external motivation and the securing of other avenues of opportunities. The landscape has shifted from a silo mentality of responsibility to a more horizontal philosophy. We have learned to leverage our assets in order to keep our jobs; grow professionally; and continue to provide excellent customer service to both internal and external clients.

We are reminded of a quote attributed to Suquamish Chief Seattle, dating to 1855: "Humankind has not woven the web of life. We are but one thread within it. Whatever we do to the web, we do to ourselves. All things are bound together. All things connect." Wearing multiple hats requires us to connect and collaborate with fellow employees in other departments. The integration of the library into other business units is the new business of law. The projects that we are working on impact other business units. It is important to understand this interconnectivity. We are vested in the same professional goals: superb customer service, excellent job performance, professional growth, and job security.

In order for us to successfully collaborate, to more effectively streamline legal services provided and/or meet client-mandated directives, we have to understand how business decisions are made and how different departments function within our organization. It is essential to speak the same language as our colleagues and be aligned to the same business goals; this can be achieved by increasing our communication, collaboration and knowledge sharing. One way to learn these critical components is through working with other departments. How do you collaborate between departments? There is no one-size-fits-all. However, some ideas to integrate library and research departments more fully into the business of law are explored below.

Start by saying "yes!"

Start with "yes!" Are you internally motivated or externally challenged? You want to be internally motivated. Pick a project that speaks to you. An example from our own practice includes being asked to contribute a chapter to this book – an opportunity to which we said yes!

It is also important to stay motivated. Research suggests that there are better outcomes associated with more engaged employees. However, employee engagement does more than boost productivity; by staying engaged employees feel like they are part of the community and that they are valued. These feelings provide employees with the initiative to be more productive, customer-focused and profit-generating than employees who are disengaged. Feeling a lack of control will contribute over time to disengagement from the employee, which is not optimal. This engagement is up to you. Any request and any opportunity should be answered with "yes"! Ensure that you go the extra mile; look for ways to solve the problem; be curious. Take the initiative and create the appearance of "can do" to foster your relationships. Create a reputation for being the "go to" person. However, it is important to not let them see you sweat – automatically say "yes" and then figure out a way to make it work. If you ultimately cannot complete the request, you will have set the stage in a positive light by responding with "yes" and can follow with a more detailed response on why a particular ask could not be completed as asked.

Communication

Take responsibility for your relationship and your communications. Have you followed up one-on-one with your attorneys or internal clients? Have you stopped by your attorney's office? Be transparent. Firm practice leaders now, more than ever, are motivated to collaborate with different departments within the company. The goal for library managers is to market the library whenever possible. Librarians collaborate with attorneys to survey the interest and needs of practice groups. Attorneys rely on librarians to conduct research, keep up with new trends in the profession, and to provide the best resources in both print or digital format. By setting up news and court docket alerts, you can help attorneys stay up to date with clients, potential clients, and areas of interest. Per attorney request, librarians handle the purchase of new databases, book titles, and subscription renewals. Practice group leaders, with the help of library managers, arrange training sessions on electronic resources. Do you know the communication style of your attorneys and partners? Some like email, some like face-to-face, while others prefer to communicate via the telephone. Take time to understand the communication preference of your team members and then follow up accordingly. Practice listening, well.

Focus on regular follow up communications with your attorneys and internal and external clients. You want to have regular touch points with your team. Did you ask how you performed on the last assignment? Did you promptly respond to the request? Did you provide a status update to your team on lengthy projects? It is important to promptly return phone calls. Did you ask if there are outstanding questions or concerns? Did you document steps taken to provide your solution? Did you offer solutions when you could not complete an assignment as requested? Have you provided information on new resources or tools? Have you provided information on professional development or training opportunities? How have you ensured the adoption of new technology or tools is more widespread?

Make yourself approachable and accessible. Walk the floors. Use the video feature on your telephone. Blog. Keep your door open. Have your five-second elevator pitch ready. Make lunch plans with fellow teammates.

It is essential to be explicit in your communication. Explain your goal (i.e. collaboration between departments) and offer suggestions on how to meet that goal. Be clear when asking questions about a particular project or opportunity. Understand what the request encompasses, and be clear when communicating your finished product.

Make sure to follow up on your project/assignment, and be willing to accept constructive feedback in order to grow. Seek regular feedback. It is also important to be mindful of the concept of "project management". Project management has emerged as a profession and many of these practices are what we have been doing all along; the difference, however, is that now we are capturing the roles and responsibilities differently. The concept of "project management" is to ensure quality and cost-effective delivery of legal services as a value add to the client services team. Make sure you are providing value.

With the emergence of multi-office collaborations, it is important to nurture "virtual" collaborations and demonstrate how one's skills can be applied beyond their department or office. Clear communication is also required. One recent example can be found within our own firm, Mayer Brown LLP, which is a multi-office, international organization. The NY office collaborated with many departments and staff – including knowledge management, paralegals, word processing and secretaries – to design and build a closing set protocol. A lot of time and energy went into building a model to be used firm-wide. The goals in designing a firm-wide protocol to follow included establishing best practice and uniformity; in addition, it would ensure that all interested parties, in any office location, would be able to locate a specific and relevant closing set. A year after starting these collaborations New York, the Chicago office undertook the same project. The New York office was required to expand upon their virtual collaboration and communication with Chicago and other offices in order to successfully implement this global practice.

Practice being a connector

We believe that librarians and research managers are adept in the "six degrees of separation" philosophy, which means that they are among a very small number of people who are linked to everyone else in a few steps. We are connectors; we have the ability and are in fact required to interact with others in different worlds. Think about how you can bridge these worlds together.

Do you know who your internal clients are? It is essential that you do, in order to facilitate collaboration between both individuals and departments. If you are a reference or research manager or librarian, some of your internal clients can be: oracles/teachers; researchers/detectives; marketers; promoters; analysts; directors/managers; customer service representatives; project managers; partners/associates; and paralegals/legal assistants, amongst others.

Knowledge management

Consider partnering with your knowledge management team. There are many areas of shared knowledge between your department and knowledge management, including but not limited to:

- Artificial intelligence (AI);
- Business intelligence strategies;
- Corporate governance;

- Standardizing forms and form management;
- Creating a forms library;
- Website creation and content;
- Intranet content development;
- Database creation;
- Jury verdict data base;
- Expert witness DBs;
- Judge DBs;
- Contract review and analysis; and
- Legal project management.

As law firms work collaboratively it opens up possibilities and enables an organization to manage, store, and share information. Librarians and research managers are working together with their firm's knowledge management department to develop practice area pages on the company homepage, for example. These practice area pages are developed to be the go-to places for new attorneys or for anyone who is looking for example documents, forms, manuals, and so on. Placing practice-specific information in one location has an enormous impact on research efficiency. This provides all employees with ease of use and the confidence to answer any questions in a timely manner. It also provides a level of assurance that they are providing the client or senior partner with accurate information, or to help answer a client's request on a practice area that is unfamiliar to the attorney.

Marketing/business development

Consider partnering with your marketing team. The joined forces of a law firm's business development and marketing team and the library department gives a firm a competitive advantage. Both departments can monitor any mention of the firm in the media and provide the attorneys with business intelligence and competitive intelligence information daily. Additional areas of shared knowledge include information to be used in RFPs, RFQs and RFIs. You could provide critical information for more competitive fee arrangements. There could be research needs for business development and general support needs for presentations and seminars, providing support at information tables during firm events.

Procurement

Consider building your relationship with procurement. The procurement department works hand-in-hand with library managers to negotiate contracts and the contract terms. Procurement reviews each vendor contract to make sure there is no hidden language, which can sometimes lead to the renegotiation of high-priced contracts and the cancellation of some resources. Before the sign-off on these contracts, librarians can compare database usage to the previous years to evaluate whether the platform is still essential to the practice. Law firms are being asked to evaluate their structure for efficiency of operation and to improve the bottom line; to save money, firms have been asked to re-evaluate all contracts, compare resources firm-wide to eliminate duplication of publications, convert from print to electronic, and to determine if there is a need to go single-sourced. Librarians can perform the research in comparing terms and prices, along with evaluating patterns of use, in order to assist procurement and boost the firm's profitability in general.

Paralegals

Attorneys work closely with paralegals and depend on them to assist with litigation support such as the preparation for hearings, closings, and trials. It is in the interest of both yourself and your firm to establish a collaborative relationship with paralegals. In fact, paralegal staff collaborate with the library just as much as associates. Paralegals help to analyze and organize legal documents; in addition, they conduct legal research such as reviewing relevant case law, keycite, and shepardizing cases. Librarians can work with paralegals on cite checking and record checking projects, briefs and documents submitted to the court. Paralegals often reach out to the library staff to assist them with various research requests, such as the retrieval of cases, patents, and articles utilizing multiple different databases and research platforms. Sometimes paralegals request more in-depth research help from the library, such as searching on Westlaw, Lexis and Bloomberg. The library can help set up docket alerts and conduct expert witness research, as well as prepare business and litigation history reports. Librarians can also help paralegals in entity searching and corporation formations. Librarians can guarantee that paralegals have their log-in credentials to access all needed resources, in addition to collaborating with them to ensure that they stay aware of all new digital resources and emailing them monthly calendar updates of all available training sessions on the different research platforms that are provided by the firm.

IT department

The IT department plays a vital role in the collaboration within law firms, guaranteeing that partners, associates, paralegals, librarians, and all other administrative staff are able to work together, whether it is via telephone, videoconference or computer network. Without the ability to conduct long-distance telephone calls and stream audio and video, attorneys – as well as other staff – will not have the capability to conduct firm-wide meetings and training sessions. It is also highly important that attorneys are able to communicate with their clients or potential clients at all times. IT departments help to facilitate the much-needed requirements to add new software to firm networks, such as library catalog systems, printers, remote access capabilities, fax, etc. IT staff can collaborate with library and research services to help develop databases to centralize each department's services. This helps to promote ways of tracking, sharing, and managing information firm-wide. Librarians and reference managers can also work with IT to make sure fire walls do not block internal client use on databases.

Proactively look for new opportunities to partner with others. Build relationships with your attorneys and your customers. Proactively seeking ways to strengthen your relationships helps you create value in your role within your organization. It identifies you as being a collaborative team member. You can also think of ways to barter your "ask" – for example, if you need a partner's approval to go forward with a particular opportunity, consider volunteering for a pet project of the partner first. Perhaps the partner is working on a marketing piece that you could help promote, or they need training for their associates. Consider setting up individual training for this group. Go out of your comfort zone, look for the opportunity, and keep in mind your ultimate goal(s).

Focus on a holistic team approach. They say that the greatest human need is to be heard. Take time to listen to the issue. Understand what the request or need is before offering a solution. Identify and utilize all stakeholders. For example, if you are trying to train a group of partners on a new technology or tool, consider training their secretary first; as the secretary gains more expertise, they can help spread the word and make sure the integration of your new tool goes more smoothly.

Do you know how to access and share information/resources within your organization? One idea is to collaborate with your librarian or research department to share information. Your librarian or research manager are a resource for many departments. Consider coordinating training through them for various databases; commonly used service providers like Lexis, Westlaw, Bloomberg; or complicated due diligence requests. Consider reaching out to them to start a research project or turn over a research project outline and request their help in going more in depth. Research alternative services and resources and suggest these resources to your firm. Consider scheduling regular meetings to discuss new tools and training.

Network

How strong is your network? Have you identified a role model or someone who can provide support to you from within your company or organization? Promote your network, accomplishments and teammates on social media. In particular, it is essential that you work to set up your teammates to win – recognize their accomplishments and help them grow. At all times keep in mind the words you use to promote others and/or strengthen your network. Your words are very important and should always be phrased in the most positive light. Your words should also follow your behavior. Accentuate the positive and catch teammates doing things right. Learn what motivates your team members. Express appreciation for a job well done. Practice gratitude for help given by others.

Trend spot

It is critical to learn to trend spot. Firm business needs have changed, and we need to understand these requirements. Structure your approach to collaboration while being cognizant of the current trends. What is the current goal of your firm or company? Are your efforts in collaboration with others aligned to this business trend or goal?

Understand what drives the client. What does the client want? Is the client determining services to be out sourced? Does the client determine how to utilize library and research assets? Does the client have a preference on who performs certain types of work? Consider participating on client calls in an observation capacity only. Some law firms have paralegals silently participate on global marketing client-specific calls. The idea behind this participation is multi-fold: the paralegal listens to the needs and requests of the client to get a better understanding of their underlying motivations; in addition, through participation in the call they better understand the focus of the work to be performed as well as who the client believes should perform certain layers of the work. Silent participation by the paralegal does not mean the paralegal dictates how work is assigned or priority of work to be completed; rather, this participation enables the paralegal to be more proactive and have a better understanding of what drives the client.

Conclusion

Librarians and reference managers are the glue that holds many law firms and corporations together. We are intimately integrated into multiple practice areas without realizing the value and significance of the roles we play, which is to help a law firm leverage its power and be successful. As librarians' roles evolve they are becoming more and more involved with business intelligence and marketing research, in order to provide the attorneys with the information they need to meet their client's expectations. All departments and staff – whether you are a librarian, paralegal or attorney – share the same goal of contributing to the firm's success. The collaborations among staff in the several different departments within a law firm are one of the major factors that ultimately make a firm a successful one.

Chapter 3:
Absorbing library services into knowledge management

By Patrick DiDomenico, chief knowledge officer at Ogletree Deakins

Formation of the knowledge management department

Although the firm had been engaging in what could be considered knowledge management activities for several years, it was not until December of 2011, when I joined as director of KM, that Ogletree Deakins formally started a knowledge management program. Here is a brief overview of how we formed the KM department.

By early 2012, we quickly formed the first iteration of our KM department by combining some existing groups, people and roles, and bringing on new people to fill the gaps. We looked across the administrative departments at the firm and identified those people who were engaging in knowledge management activities, even if those activities were by another name.

First was a senior-manager-level team member who, 25 years earlier, had been responsible for establishing and running the library. Her activities in 2012 focused on building out the firm's first SharePoint-based intranet platform and attempting to organize the firm's administrative information in a way that was easily accessible. Within a few months – by mid-2012 – we brought on others (including a former colleague of mine at my prior firm) to help these efforts, and together that group formed what we currently call the KM firm solutions group.

Next was a long-standing practice support group. This team was originally charged with responsibilities related to managing and supporting large client engagements. This included custom reporting and making client information accessible via an extranet platform. This group, which consisted of about four members, went on to be reorganized and renamed what we currently call the KM client solutions group.

A new role for the firm was practice support lawyer, otherwise known as knowledge management attorney. With the impending formation of the KM department, a shareholder in the firm indicated interest in transitioning from practicing lawyer to practice support lawyer. He joined the KM department immediately in December 2011 as our first KM counsel, focusing on identifying and organizing substantive legal documents and helping the practicing lawyers understand and apply knowledge management to their practices. By mid-2012, we had brought on a second KM counsel.

The final group that made up our nascent KM department, which is the focus of this chapter, is the library services group (LSG). Because of the natural fit with knowledge management, the LSG became a part of the KM department immediately upon its formation. This was the largest and most well-established group in the KM department, as the firm had had a library (in one form or another) since around the time of its founding in 1977. Up until joining the KM department, the library staff had grown with the firm since and, by the end of 2011, totaled approximately 15 members, including a senior manager who had been in the role for several years.

Since library services was the most well-established group, and had been operating well for several years, the main focus of the new KM department during the first few years of its existence was building out the fundamental components of a modern KM program. Without dwelling on the details, this meant spending the majority of our time on five areas: rounding out the KM department with additional staff; establishing and improving processes and procedures; implementing an enterprise search platform; creating a modern (and ultimately award-winning) SharePoint-based intranet platform; and implementing a robust, modern extranet collaboration platform.

Evolution of the library – an objective look

A few years after establishing the primary KM functions of the knowledge management department, in 2015 we shifted our focus to the library group and took a fresh, objective look at it. While the library had been performing well for many years, the question was whether we could improve performance and reduce the cost of providing top-notch service.

By way of additional background, the following is a closer look at the structure of the library group at the time. At a high level, the library was divided in two subgroups: technical services and reference librarians. The technical services group consisted of eight members with the titles "technical services librarian" or "technical services assistant," depending on roles and functions. The reference librarian subgroup consisted of five reference librarians who reported to a reference manager. Both subgroups reported to the senior manager of library services, who reported to myself as director of knowledge management. Most members of the library group were located in our Greenville administrative office in South Carolina, but some members of the group were based in one of our various offices around the country.

When I decided to focus on the library to assess whether changes were appropriate, I started to question all aspects of the library and librarianship, in general. For several years, reports from the legal industry press indicated that libraries and library budgets were shrinking. I had had first-hand experience with that at other firms at which I served in KM roles. Some progressive library and information professional thinkers called for the end of "the L words," suggesting that "library" and "librarian" conjured up images of dusty old rooms filled with books and curmudgeonly, bespectacled "shooshers." I knew that these stereotypes (at least the latter) were inaccurate. Librarians – by any name – provide an incredibly valuable service that should not be marginalized. On the contrary, it should be lauded. However, I also knew that perception is incredibly important when it comes to promoting a team and the services it provides.

As with all such inquiries, I tried to be as empathetic as possible. I reminded myself of a mantra I try to observe when considering options: we are not them. More specifically, we (KM and library professionals) are not them (the attorneys we serve). We needed to be careful to not assume that that which we value and desire is the same as that of our lawyers. My gut feeling – which was likely a remnant of my days as practicing as a litigation attorney a decade earlier – was that libraries and librarians did, in some instances, have a bad reputation among lawyers. It's unfair and inaccurate, but reputations are not a matter of fact; they are a matter of opinion. We needed to do what we could to improve the perception and reputation of the people who provided the excellent and valuable services that our library group did.

I challenged my team to look at things with the goal of improving the services we deliver to our lawyers and clients without regard to structure, position, job titles, or other historical constraints. What if we could do anything? What if money was not a concern? What if we could make any changes we wanted to make? What if we could make an entirely new thing? What would it look like? Who would do what, and how?

"Nothing is sacred," I told my team. This is another mantra that I have valued for many years. When you hold something sacred, you never think beyond it. You never challenge it. You never question it. Holding something sacred limits your possibilities. It automatically excludes certain options. Declaring that "nothing is sacred" breaks down those limits and eliminates barriers that you once thought were insurmountable. When you eliminate the artificial restrictions that – for whatever reason – you believe are impossible to challenge, your mind will open to vast possibilities.

This exercise was useful because it did, in fact, generate new and exciting ideas. In reality, we knew that we couldn't really do *anything*. We knew that money was, in fact, a concern. However, the exercise alone broadened our thinking. Even with the constraints of budget and firm structure, we arrived at a place in our thinking that might not have otherwise been possible.

The end result and how we got there

After months of study, exploration, and feedback from the library staff, our lawyers, and other members of the firm, we came up with a preliminary plan – a restructuring of the library services group. However, to help ensure we were doing the right thing, we needed fresh eyes on the ideas we developed. As a check on our preliminary ideas, we hired an outside consultancy to perform an assessment. They took an objective deep dive into our library operations and listed several suggested improvements. Knowing of our preliminary suggestion to restructure, they confirmed that our plans were viable and, in fact, that the changes should improve service delivery, efficiency, morale, and overall performance of the library services group.

Our approach to the restructuring plan was based on empathy. We took a detailed, objective look at the library services group and the roles within it. We talked with each member of the staff to understand what they actually did on a daily basis. When we did that, the first thing that became clear was the terms "library" and "librarian" didn't really apply or resonate with most of our customers (our lawyers). For example, what did reference librarians actually do? Did they refer lawyers to answers and resources? True or not, the term "reference librarian" was – to most non-librarians – an antiquated and mysterious term. To oversimplify the answer, for all practical purposes, they performed mostly legal research for attorneys. It seemed, then, that we should give them a title that more accurately described their function. We settled on "legal researcher." While this may seem simplistic, and perhaps obvious, it required thought and consideration of multiple parties. How would the reference librarians feel about it? Would it make sense to the attorneys? Did it somehow conflict with other titles in the firm? While there was some disagreement and some reluctance to change titles at all (e.g. "We've always called them reference librarians, why should we change now?"), the change was overwhelmingly welcomed. Not only did it make more sense because of the descriptive nature, but it also seemed to invigorate our team of legal researchers.

The other subgroup within the library services group was a little more challenging because their titles, roles, and daily activities varied more than those of the legal researchers. The existing titles "technical services librarian" and "technical services assistant" were complete mysteries to our lawyers. (e.g. "What does 'technical services' mean? Are they part of the IT department?"). Again, from the lawyers' perspectives, the library provided research services. Rarely, if ever, did lawyers interact with technical services librarians or assistants. Of course, we in the KM department knew that the technical services librarians and assistants provided very valuable services; that was without question. However, to our customers, it caused confusion.

While some may argue that this is not an issue, I disagree because I have seen the damage that such confusion and misunderstanding can cause. Remember that perception is important. At a previous firm, for example, the senior management team to which I reported intensely questioned the value of the technical services group because they did not understand it: "What is a technical services librarian, anyway? You have *how many* people in this role? I've never even heard of them! What do they do all day? Do we really even need them or can we get rid of them?" Beware: there is little light between obscurity and obsolescence.

At Ogletree, we decided that the best titles for this group would mirror the already established and reputable titles in the KM firm solutions group. In fact, not only would the titles be the same, but the groups would merge as a part of the restructuring. More accurately, the library technical services group was absorbed into the KM firm solutions group. After the detailed evaluation of the functions and daily activities of the two groups, this made perfect sense. We realized that there was significant overlap in the roles and duties. Without getting into too much detail, the daily tasks ranged from administrative functions, such as vendor invoice processing, to quasi-research tasks, such as obtaining copies of complaints, and case law in response to lawyer requests. Another area of focus for some members of this group was reporting of KM department metrics and performance. Merging the two groups – technical services and KM firm solutions – also allowed them to work more closely together and cross-train. This expanded the functions of many members of the group and ultimately made their roles more valuable and fulfilling.

Another benefit of absorbing the technical services subgroup into KM firm solutions was the consolidation of reporting lines and management. For several years, the senior manager of the KM firm solutions group had been doing a great job; by expanding her team and adding the technical services group, we realized even greater efficiencies and benefits. The team became tighter, more streamlined, and capable. We were also able to promote a member of the team to a supervisory role, which helped with managing the work of the larger team. Ultimately, the former technical services staff members adopted titles of KM firm solutions analysts and assistants, depending on their levels.

We instituted a similar structural (reporting line) change with the newly-minted legal researchers (formerly reference librarians). Under the previous model, the reference librarians reported to a reference manager. However, our assessment revealed that the work of previously-mentioned KM counsel group and the now-called legal researchers was similar in many ways. While legal researchers mainly focused on resources that were outside the firm, typically provided by vendors such as Westlaw and Lexis, the KM counsel team focused on internal resources, such as our matter and precedent documents. While the content came from different places, the activities around the content (research and guidance) was almost identical. Since legal researchers and KM counsel had such similar functional duties, we decided to consolidate the reporting lines under the senior KM counsel manager. As was the case with the consolidation on the KM firm solutions side, this enabled the research and KM counsel groups to work more closely together, collaborate, and learn from each other. As with the KM firm solutions group, we also promoted a member of the team to a supervisory role, which helped with management.

Lessons learned

While the overall project to absorb the library services group in to the KM department went well, we learned many lessons from the experience. The most important lesson was about the human impact of change management. Even though we knew that the changes would be difficult, they were even more challenging than we expected. As with most changes, the real challenges are people challenges. We learned that you can never communicate enough about such big changes. The structure and reporting lines and job descriptions are relatively easy, but understanding that people get emotional about such changes requires attention and patience. It helps to be open and transparent about the proposed changes and, most importantly, about *why* the changes are needed. I have found over the years that most of the challenges surrounding change comes from the feeling of being excluded and not being advised of the *reasons* for the changes. Sharing these helps calm fears and promotes understanding.

Probably the most important aspect of dealing with change management is to listen. Listening to your team members is key to helping everyone deal with changes. When people are able to express their concerns and ask questions openly, they tend to feel more comfortable. The added benefit is that quite often, as was the case with our efforts, team members will raise issues or make points that we failed to consider.

Conclusion

The foregoing has been a description, not a prescription. It was the right plan and decision for our firm, but it may not be right for yours. There are so many factors at play in such big-picture decisions that a single approach will never work for all organizations. I am happy to report that two-and-a-half years after the transition began, the new structure continues to work well. We have made slight revisions over that period and will likely continue to do so. As with all such endeavors, this has transitioned from a project into an ever-evolving process.

Chapter 4:
Proactive research and anticipatory intelligence

By Scott D Bailey, global research services director at Squire Patton Boggs, and David Kamien, CEO of Mind-Alliance Systems

The relentless need for business development (BD) intelligence: a major challenge for law firms

Law firm libraries and research services departments have always played a critical role in law firm business success. They support the business development (BD) team and practices by helping maintain current awareness about industries and providing information about clients' and prospects' business and risk environment. However, as the competition for legal services increases, two new types of capabilities are increasingly required: (1) proactive support, which means that librarians and researchers initiate research before an attorney or BD staff member requests it; and (2) anticipatory intelligence, which identifies events and trends that may cause a client or prospect to require legal services in the future.

An increasing number of library departments realize that they must increase their value to the firm by moving from being reactive to proactive in finding new business opportunities for the firm. However, doing so requires process improvement and change management. Some researchers are not accustomed to taking a highly proactive approach to information gathering. They may not see it as their role to anticipate business development opportunities and initiate research.

The nexus between research services and new business development is changing rapidly due to competition and technology evolution. It is no longer enough to respond to research requests. Research teams must now capture knowledge about clients and prospects by proactively conducting research, producing new kinds of alerts and newsletters, utilizing the best eResources and building predictive models. They need to proactively deliver BD research products designed for specific practice areas, types of attorneys, regions, and types of matters. If they wait until the law firm receives an RFP or an attorney requests BD-related research, they have waited too long.

Library and research services directors are increasingly aware that they need to continually optimize their capabilities, across people, process, technology, data and governance to enable their firms to spot emerging opportunities, win a larger percentage of them, and develop closer attorney-client relationships that ultimately deliver more value to clients.

Why aren't some law firm research departments already making these changes? Because those firms face many fundamental challenges, including the following:

Research requests from attorneys and BD staff submitted in an unplanned, ad-hoc manner

Law firms do not have procedures or systems in place to automatically trigger research requests when certain market, regulatory, legal or client-onboarding events occur. Relying on BD staff or lawyers to remember to request BD research is inefficient and unreliable.

Limitations to current staffing, strategies, and scale

Law firms vary widely in their research analysis capability. In small firms, attorneys may do their own research; in multinational firms, entire research staffs may be available. Some law firms outsource research and analysis. While some law firms have dramatically increased their BD research headcount in recent years, some have reduced their research librarian staffs. Firms are struggling to keep up with the fast pace of intelligence development, and how best to stay on top of it may present quite a challenge to them.

An overwhelming workload of research requests

In some firms, the core research processes are not able to keep up with demand, and need to be improved before research can become more proactive and sophisticated. Some law firm research teams are so overwhelmed by the volume of requests that they currently receive that they find it difficult to imagine become more proactive.

Loss of institutional knowledge

When firms' most experienced researchers, librarians and analysts leave or retire, valuable institutional knowledge is at risk of being lost. Piecing together an understanding of BD research support needs from historical email communications after the fact is difficult.

The bottom line is that law firm libraries and research teams should become more proactive in supporting BD, but they are often distracted by day-to-day priorities; they need help making this transition. So what can law firms do to prepare themselves to meet the challenges of the new business development environment? How do they transition from becoming reactive to proactive? The first step in understanding how to become more proactive and help BD to anticipate events that drive demand for legal services is to examine past research requests and understand their context.

Transitioning from reactivity to proactivity

Law firms can meet the demands for BD research support more effectively by transitioning from being reactive to being proactive. Specifically, here are the steps to making this transition:

1. Thoroughly assess the existing BD research resources and processes;
2. Encourage all staff members to be more proactive about supporting BD;
3. Analyze past and current research requests to discern patterns;
4. Apply business intelligence analytics to your current "ticketing" system;
5. Retrain your library and research staff members;
6. Optimize your understanding of your clients' needs; and
7. Standardize all your firm's procedures, practices, and research products.

STEP 1: Assess the resources and functional areas you already have at your firm

All law libraries need a framework for systematically analyzing their core capabilities – the people, process, technology, and data – involved in library and research activities relevant to supporting business development. Here are some example components of this analysis process:

- Monitor research support capabilities, with an emphasis on current and predictive awareness;
- Review your firm's subscription information products and services, especially going beyond those generally available; and
- Train new associates and staff on research methods and systems.

Your assessment will provide answers to the following key questions:

- How do people, internal and external to the firm, perceive the firm's current processes?
- How well documented are current processes and procedures?
- What would be the ideal process?
- What is standing in the way of this ideal capability being realized?
- What obstacles are in place that currently impede the flow of information?
- What is the current division of responsibility and activities among departments; is it optimized?
- Are we under-utilizing expensive data resources?
- How are we currently matching research needs to resource guides and e-resources; would automation allow us to do a better job?
- How are analysts using the e-resources we have; are they taking full advantage of these resources?
- Do we have the right human resources?
- Do we have enough analysts in the right places?
- Are we fully utilizing the people we do have available?
- Should we outsource? If so, what?
- Are we matching requests to the optimal people?

Process diagrams help to identify interventions that will enhance collaboration and improve outcomes. Process maps can graphically depict library business processes and the flow of information among organizations, roles, tasks, decisions, and IT. These artifacts can facilitate discussions about feedback loops and other dimensions of the socio-technical system-of-systems.

All libraries would benefit by periodically stepping back and systematically evaluating how well they support the firm's business priorities, and to what degree they are contributing to the firm's desire to identify attractive business growth opportunities.

STEP 2: Encourage all staff members to be more proactive about new business development

The concept of "anticipatory intelligence" may be new to many attorneys, researchers, and librarians. The term refers to the ability to characterize and reduce uncertainty by providing decision makers with timely and accurate forecasts of significant global events. Beyond monitoring news about past events and current contexts, proactive law firms collect and analyze information about possible future events that might expose current and prospective clients to risk. At the same time, because these possible future events pose a risk to clients, they also provide an opportunity for practice groups. Successfully anticipating these events enables library and research directors, client development, practice group chairs and development managers to prepare accordingly.

Questions that researchers/librarians can ask to avoid missing business development opportunities for the firm are as follows:

- Are we helping the firm focus its business development efforts effectively?
- Are we prioritizing business development-related research projects strategically?
- Are we proactively spotting business development opportunities before other firms do?
- Are we able to identify meaningful industry patterns and insights, or do they go unobserved?
- Are we providing strategic guidance to all firm and practice groups, especially insofar as it relates to business development?

These complex questions can only be addressed through effective collaboration involving chief marketing officers, business development directors, and library/research departments.

The need for expertise in anticipatory intelligence gathering cannot be over-emphasized, and law firms need to have access to expertise in this area. Indeed, compiling useful intelligence in order to profile a company is more than just a "fill-in-a template" exercise. A good company profile or background report outlines a company's business initiatives and global activities in a way that reveals potential needs for legal services. For example, when the M&A team requests a company profile about a Chinese public company that invests in the U.S. tech sector, an experienced research analyst should know that specific government ownership and certain transactions queries would trigger a review by the Committee on Foreign Investment in the United States (CFIUS).

Research systems that are powered by artificial intelligence and that use advanced analytics are coming to the legaltech market. They will transform the way law firms focus business development efforts, ensuring that they direct their attention on the right industries, companies, and opportunities. Research directors can help shape the design of these systems and prioritize the integration of data sources.

STEP 3: Analyze the firm's historical and current research requests

Law firm research departments receive tens of thousands of research requests via email each year. These research requests and their resolutions result in valuable data that not only help optimize the research department's internal processes but also accelerate the productivity of librarians and research analysts.

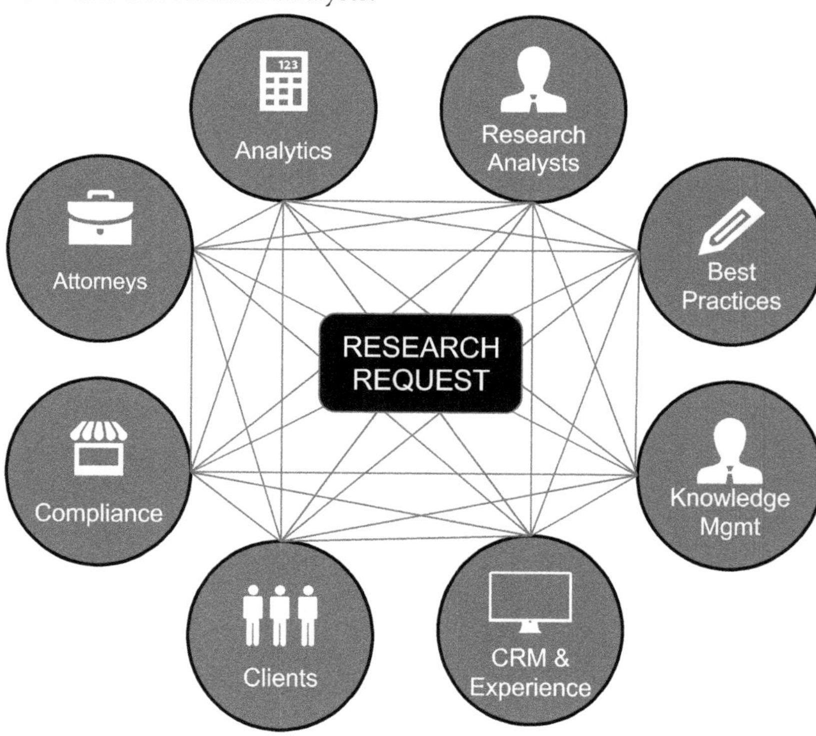

Figure 1: Research request map

Few firms are equipped to exploit this expanding universe of information systematically. With the right software tools and methods, law firms can analyze these emails to spot business development indicators and client development opportunities.

Technologies such as natural language processing (NLP), machine learning (ML), process mining, and information visualization can help libraries find meaningful patterns in past and current research requests. For example, the library may see that multiple attorneys are asking about the same new regulation that has potential to impact an entire industry. Marketing teams and lawyers can then write thought leadership content about this topic, proactively providing clients with timely guidance before they even request it.

STEP 4: Take a business intelligence approach to handling your firm's "ticketing" system

Ticketing systems of all types are used to prioritize and triage research requests. Libraries often develop a taxonomy of research request types and systematize the production of the most common types; this not only accelerates research analyst productivity but also increases the efficient utilization of e-resources.

However, how do you create a proactive ticketing system? How do you turn a reactive system into a proactive one?

As always, the first step is to see what you already have and ask yourself questions about the current system:

- Which attorneys send research requests to specific analysts? A decline in requests from lawyer A to research analyst B might indicate that the lawyer experienced poor service.
- Which staff members are available to respond to requests and at what times? Does the current staffing align with spikes in research requests?
- How many research requests does the firm get annually, monthly, by practice group, by location, by request type?
- What is the average time to resolution by request type and by researcher?
- How many go unresolved? More specifically, what percentage of requests go unresolved?
- How many analysts are needed per number of requests? What is a suitable "case load" for an analyst?
- Which individual research email inboxes get how many research requests, and from whom?

- Which teams inside the research departments handle the most research requests?
- What are the trends in the growth or decline of requests in each practice area?
- Does the firm pay its employees overtime in order to handle the number of requests that come in?

Knowing the answers to these questions allows the firm to re-shape and optimize its ticketing system, maximizing the potential for staff to respond to additional, more proactive requests.

STEP 5: Train library/research staff

Training is critical to improving the ability of library staff to meet new business development intelligence needs. Library staff can learn to use structured analytic techniques, for example, for forecasting events. These kinds of tools can free up researchers to focus on proactive intelligence collection and analysis in the following areas:

- Knowledge management;
- Human and machine integration;
- Semantic data management through the use of virtual knowledge graphs (understanding the relationships among data points); and
- BD leadership development (including information sharing and effective collaboration).

Curating news feeds and producing newsletters are time-consuming processes. Not surprisingly, many librarians find themselves reacting to requests from attorneys who want them to set up alerts, as opposed to proactively suggesting to attorneys that the library set them up. For example, when a new bill is passed in Congress and has the potential to impact clients, the researcher has an opportunity to provide an alert to the relevant practice group proactively. Industry groups and BD teams deeply appreciate proactive action that can result in awareness about new business opportunities.

Librarians also need data about whether alert emails are opened and read, and what feedback is received about their relevance and usefulness. They especially need to know which deliverables resulted in actionable business development intelligence and led to new business.

Unfortunately, current awareness and media monitoring software tools cannot consistently deliver high-value alerts on autopilot with "set-and-forget" configurations. It is therefore not enough for librarians to "police" the newsfeeds, tweak search parameters, and manually check that the retrieved articles appear to be relevant.

In today's information-driven law firm, researchers and librarians are required to systematically measure the utility, relevance, and value of alerts and newsletters from the perspective of recipients (e.g., attorneys and BD staff); they also need to be able to measure engagement levels. The lightning speed of information puts intense pressure on research staff, but that's not the only challenge. It is essential for staff members to interact with patrons to elicit feedback and to find out how to improve.

STEP 6: Do you really fully understand your client's needs?

Librarians and research analysts need to partner with practice groups, industry teams and associated business development professionals to fully understand relevant business development opportunities. Together, they can identify the types of events that may trigger opportunities and – more importantly – indicators that these events might occur in the future. For example, negative social media sentiment about a product or experience with a service provider could be a leading indicator of an eventual product liability lawsuit. Stock price movements and insider trades could indicate potential opportunities for securities fraud litigation work.

STEP 7: Standardize BD research products and services

Law firm libraries can design templates for the firm's most commonly requested business development research products and services. These can become "standard research products" that lawyers and business development staff can easily order online. Examples include:

- **News briefs/newsletters/bulletins**. Current awareness news monitoring that leverages automatic summarization. Daily or weekly intelligence briefs cover topics, trends, and developments related to the law, government policy, regulation, industry developments, litigation, markets, and the economy.
- **Opportunity alert emails**. When analysts spot a potential opportunity in a news article within the stream, they can complete a suitable business development opportunity template.

- **Business background reports, memos and briefing books**. These products contain automatically integrated information from business and legal subscription resources about companies and industries; analysts would no longer need to copy and paste manually.
- **People profiles**. Profiles of executives, general counsels, in-house counsel, opposing counsel, and legislators. Profiles can aggregate forward-looking statements about their business priorities, mergers and acquisitions (M&A) transactions, proposed regulations, and technology.
- **List of events and attendee**. Highlighting the most relevant conferences and other types of events for showcasing thought leadership and networking with executives.
- **Contact information**. For the chief of staff (CoS), legislative director (LD), or scheduler, for example.
- **Industry profiles**. Providing details on the following:
    - What is the firm's relationship with government X?
    - What is the firm's experience with deal type X?
    - Description of an industry;
    - Lists of companies in an industry;
    - Lists of industry subject matter experts;
    - Which clients has lawyer X represented and in which cases?
    - Business relationships and corporate trees; and
    - Copy of an article.

Conclusion

This chapter has identified key challenges law firms face in dealing with the unrelenting flow of BD research requests, along with strategies to meet these challenges head-on. The emphasis is on transitioning from a reactive to a proactive law firm in order to optimize the firm's new business development opportunities. Fundamentally, libraries and research teams can power business development growth by enhancing their firm's understanding of clients' needs. Providing timely, accurate, and relevant anticipatory intelligence to business development teams gives law firms a competitive edge.

Chapter 5: How law firm professionals can make an impact on practice-orientated legal education

By Jocelyn K Sagherian, reference librarian at the Maloney Library of the Fordham University School of Law

As I write this chapter, 3Ls across the land are donning caps and gowns for law school graduation. Most will study and then take the bar exam for their respective states. Subsequently, thousands will assume their positions as first-year associates in law firms. Some will be confident, believing that with their newly-minted law degrees, coupled with their innate talent, they are ready for anything a large law firm can throw their way. Some will be crippled with anxiety, sure they are not prepared for the myriad challenges they are about to face. As an informational professional at a law firm who has presumably been through this cycle before, which students do you think are right?[1]

Based on the sheer amount of blog posts and articles dedicated to the topic, I believe the general consensus is that law students, upon graduation, are not prepared to engage in the modern practice of law. This encompasses both students' technological preparedness as well as their understanding of the business of legal practice. This can lead to a delay in meaningful contributions by new associates and frequently fed-up clients. The response to this problem – or even agreement as to whether this is a problem at all – has varied widely between and within law schools. In addition to reviewing some of the trends and individual approaches taken by law schools around the country, this chapter will discuss ways law firm librarians can assist in this new approach to legal education with the goal of improving the bottom line of the law firm.

What's the problem?

In recent decades, law schools were not required to prepare students for the mechanics of actual practice. The firms were expected to provide new associates with the training they needed to perform their day-to-day duties while simultaneously billing clients for the time. This all changed with the recession and the resulting adjustment in client expectations. Clients are less inclined to pay for untrained lawyers and can look to other sources within this competitive market, be that other firms or alternative legal services providers. In response, some firms have created intensive training programs that go well beyond the traditional orientation for their new hires, such as the one recently rolled out by Morrison & Foerster called MoFo University.[2] While undoubtedly helpful, this type of extensive immersion takes away from potential billable time from these new associates, not to mention absorbing resources from other areas of the firm. I would also argue that this contributes substantially to new associates' anxiety, as it slowly dawns on them how little of what they learned in law school prepared them for actual practice.

Accordingly, there is an argument that more practice and technology-oriented training should be implemented during law school, when students are paying to learn rather than being paid. This notion has not fully resonated throughout the legal education community. Recently, I overheard a tenured faculty member engaged in a general discussion on the merits of teaching legal technology skills to students in law school. "What's the point?" he said. "They'll just learn it at their law firms." This attitude is pervasive amongst those who by and large hold the power over the law school curriculum.

Why is this the case? Mark A. Cohen (distinguished fellow at Northwestern University Pritzker School of Law) has laid out some potential reasons:

> *"1) the detachment of most law schools from the marketplace;*
> *(2) tenured faculty's characteristic absence of practice experience;*
> *(3) a 'business as usual' approach to legal education when that no longer cuts it;*
> *(4) a widespread misconception—especially among top-tier law schools—that the conveyor belt that carried a majority of graduates into large firms is balky but not about to break;*
> *(5) failure to grasp that legal 'practice' is shrinking while legal operations and the business of law is expanding—law schools teach almost exclusively for practice careers; and*
> *(6) failure to provide more full-time faculty positions for those with practice experience and different backgrounds than the pedigree-centric, narrowly tailored Law Review, clerkship, and academic career paths of most tenured faculty."*[3]

For these reasons, most of legal education encompasses substantially the same techniques as when Christopher Columbus Langdell promoted the caselaw method in the late nineteenth and early twentieth centuries at Harvard Law School.[4] In short, students are required to read legal cases and answer questions designed to develop their ability to "think like a lawyer." This method serves as the backbone for most first-year legal classes and for many substantive upper-level courses as well.

This is of course not the only pedagogical method used in law schools. ABA accreditation now requires that a law school offer substantial "live-client or other real-life practice experience" for students to complete their mandated "experiential" learning requirement. Legal clinics are a common experiential offering at law schools. While there have been ebbs and flows in its popularity, clinical legal education has been around almost as long as the caselaw method. The modern legal clinic emerged in the 1960s, and the number of law school clinics have increased dramatically in recent decades.[5]

While clinical education does provide students with certain practice-oriented legal experiences, this does not necessarily translate into the type of training needed for large law. To start, participation in a clinic is optional at most law schools. Additionally, while not exclusively so, most clinics are litigation-focused (although there has been an uptick in the number of transactional clinics). The litigation is mostly of a very different type than that found in a large law firm. Clinic participants are rarely dealing with large e-discovery requests or employing legal analytics to determine likelihood of success. For the most part, they are not formally taught methodical ways to access and organize information within their organization. They are not thinking about billing or business development.

This doesn't mean that they couldn't be. In fact, there are many opportunities within the clinic to introduce these concepts and get students into a more technology and business-focused mindset. Further, clinics are only one of the many opportunities within a law school where this type of education can take place. This, however, speaks to the larger question: how much technology and business-oriented training should be introduced at the law school level, and who is responsible for its implementation? Currently, law schools are answering this question in wildly varying ways.

The basic versus the cool

Part of the hesitation of law schools to jump into this world of legal technology and practice-oriented training, I think, is the difficulty of defining what exactly this means. First, you have actual tools, including the Microsoft Office Suite, various types of software (such as that used for e-discovery and legal practice management), and mobile platforms. It is a massive understatement to state that this is not an exhaustive list. There are also newer, somewhat amorphous skill sets, such as performing business development research, analyzing legal analytics, and understanding legal project management. Additionally, there are the burgeoning areas, such as artificial intelligence and blockchain, which increasingly threaten to change the practice of law as we know it.

In a recent post, Ken Grady (adjunct professor and research fellow at Michigan State University College of Law) muses over what would be the optimal level of technology training for today's students. He writes:

> *"The debate rages today over what level of tech training law schools should provide to law students. Others debate how tech knowledgeable practicing lawyers must become. At one end, some law schools are teaching how to code artificial intelligence and machine learning. At the other end, many law schools are ignoring tech. We also have schools teaching specific legal tech software and others teaching basic skills."*[6]

Putting aside for a moment those schools that are "ignoring tech" completely, Grady's statement essentially encompasses what I have come to think of as "the basic versus the cool." Certain schools are wholly embracing classes on machine learning and coding, building new platforms for legal service delivery, and innovating new ways to look at big data. This is what I consider "the cool," but it can be intimidating to those in the law school community without a background in this area. While Grady recognizes the value of these programs, he argues that these may not be the best approach for every school or the best type of training for every lawyer. He maintains that teaching certain tools of the trade – such as word processing/spreadsheet/presentation, research, and other essential legal software – is perhaps a better use of limited law student time at most institutions. This is what I have dubbed "the basic." There is value for both types of education, but it can be a useful framework for law schools as they seek to allocate resources.

So, what is actually happening at law schools throughout the country? A good place to begin is the Law School Innovation Index.[7] This is a project helmed by Michigan State University College of Law and is an attempt to catalog law school innovation and technology programs. Using a graphical interface, the user can see programs, legal service delivery disciplines, and legal service delivery courses available at a specific school.

While I do not think this gives an entirely comprehensive account of every school (and certainly does not guarantee what each individual student is taught while there), this index can be a helpful starting point in determining how much a law school is committed to incorporating technology and legal practice skills into its curriculum. For example, some standout schools for legal technology and innovation are Michigan State University, Chicago-Kent, and Suffolk law schools. Grady discusses some of these schools in his post, citing their focus on machine learning labs and coding. However, the index fails to note some of the most interesting things happening at law schools that can be categorized as "the basic." One example is the Oklahoma University School of Law's Digital Initiative.[8] This program offers biweekly lunchtime trainings on topics related to legal technology and practice, and students are mandated to attend a designated number throughout the school year.[9] Offerings include – among other options – extensive Microsoft Office, legal practice, and case management software training. I believe this program is the current gold standard for the "basic" type of training advocated by Grady.

Crucially, Grady maintains that legal tools should be used to illustrate concepts and cement skills that are transferable across platforms. Except for Microsoft Office software, which I think is still ubiquitous in legal practice, I wholly agree with this viewpoint.[10] It would not be efficient to train individual students on every possible piece of software they could conceivably encounter at their specific firms. Even if we were to devise a way, these tools change too quickly for point-and-click-here training to be of much use. Rather, the goal is to give students a framework for whatever software they encounter during practice.

Once a law school has decided whether to move towards the basic, the cool, or towards a combination of both, the next step is to decide who is going to teach it. There are a number of possibilities. As discussed, clinics are an excellent place to introduce legal practice management and process. Another popular method is to bring in adjunct professors to teach. In many ways, adjuncts are the exact opposite of most tenured faculty; they are generally practicing lawyers enmeshed in the current conditions of the market. Like clinical professors, however, adjunct professors are rarely afforded the same prestige as tenured faculty and tenured faculty's classes. Students may accordingly perceive these classes as less important than doctrinal classes. More concerningly, adjuncts often have other commitments and are generally under no obligation to teach from one semester to the next. This can lead to inconsistencies in course offerings and leave students with unmet educational needs.

Law school librarians are also leading the efforts to introduce legal technology and practice classes and trainings. These offerings take many different forms, but there are certain areas of legal technology that fall right in line with most teaching librarians' existing skill sets. A prime example is selecting and navigating both the increasing number of legal analytics and research platforms incorporating artificial intelligence. In addition to understanding how to use this information in practice, the sites must also be evaluated for authority, credibility, currency, and reliability (including bias) – all principles of information literacy that librarians have long taught. Librarians have also taught eDiscovery (essentially, an electronic document production creates a large, searchable database – another area of librarian expertise). Additionally, librarians can be very effective at teaching the mechanics of business development research. This is just a small sampling of what is occurring at law school libraries.

Finally, there is the option to bring in outside experts. Even for librarians and adjuncts, it is difficult to keep up with the constantly evolving state of legal technology. As a supplement, it can be very helpful to bring in specialists in specific areas, particularly in areas such as artificial intelligence and blockchain, to provide background and context for students. This can include alumni or vendors with access to different tools and platforms.[11] If a vendor is brought in, however, it is important that they are not just marketing their product or doing a point-and-click training as referenced above.[12]

Regardless of who is offering the training and how the law school chooses to offer it, one of the biggest obstacles to getting a critical mass of students trained is getting bodies in the seats (or in front of their computers, if choosing a virtual approach). This is more of a challenge than it would appear. There is often resistance to this type of education by faculty, as detailed above. Additionally, having no encouragement to the contrary, many students prioritize taking class subjects that also appear on the bar exam. Without discounting the importance of doctrinal classes in legal education, this necessarily takes away from classes on subjects of technology and legal practice. Finally, even if these trainings are offered outside of formal classes, those of us engaged in this work are competing for precious student time. This is similar to the challenges law school librarians have historically faced with legal research course offerings and class trainings. With no mandate from the administration, it is difficult to convince students to make learning these skills a priority.

What's a law firm information professional to do?

Steps have certainly been taken throughout the country to modernize legal education. We are not going to radically change the established tradition overnight, and there are plenty of arguments against doing so. However, if you – as a law firm professional – are in the camp that believes law schools can and should do more to create practice-ready graduates, what follows are some suggestions on how you can assist in the process.

Encourage your vendors to create meaningful training tools for law schools

I have already discussed the importance on not focusing too much on specific tools. Nevertheless, access to various legal technology platforms is a crucial component to give students a hands-on experience where they can implement what they learn. I am speaking of programs that go well beyond the traditional vendor training where someone from marketing shows up to do a product demonstration. For example, in my most recent course, I relied on two relatively new vendor programs to give students hands-on, practice-oriented experience. The first was Clio University, which allowed my students to practice case management and billing. I also used Catalyst's E-discovery Practicum, where students were able to simulate a document review and production. Law school programs like these garners the vendors little to no profit. They make their money, of course, from law firms' purchases. As information professionals who sign these contracts (or work closely with those who do), I urge you to use your buying power to encourage this type of access. If there is a certain skill you see lacking in your current crop of associates, reach out to the vendor that supplies this at your firm and encourage them to innovate a law school program. It would be particularly helpful if the program could be flexible in how it is offered – a professor may have an entire semester to teach eDiscovery, or she may have two hours. Bonus points if they can make it free!

Communicate with your summer associates on what you think is important

While you cannot make sweeping generalizations about all law students, I think it is safe to assume that most want to begin their careers as prepared as possible. Unless told otherwise, they mostly believe this involves taking class subjects that appear on the bar exam, coupled with substantive classes in their future practice areas. Consider investigating what legal technology course options or supplemental trainings are available at the top feeder schools for your firm and decide if you think these would be helpful for incoming associates. Encourage your 2L summer associates to take the legal technology and practice-oriented courses available at their schools. If law school administrators are to be convinced that this is a vital part of legal education, it will be because students vote with their enrollment and oversubscribe. You are in a unique position to influence this outcome.

Advocate publicly for specific skills you'd like to see to taught in law schools

As previously discussed, there are many articles and posts written by legal professionals about students' lack of preparedness for practice. However, most of these pieces tend towards general statements rather than offering detailed recommendations. Sharing specific ideas on which skillsets would be valuable for new associates would be very helpful to the academic community. For example, instead of saying students should learn the business of law, the article could discuss how practicing time tracking and billing is a helpful exercise. The article could even go as far as suggesting how these skills could be practiced at the law school level. Ideally, the author would share examples of new associates who were better equipped to succeed because of training they received (or, conversely, associates who were not prepared, and what would have been helpful to them). These pieces can serve as evidence to the administration of the need for this type of education and are particularly valuable when a large law firm's name is attached. Further, they give academics a better idea of where to focus their energies. Overall, this is an excellent way to communicate your firm's needs to those in a position to make changes.

Reach out to your counterparts at your biggest feeder schools

While articles and blog posts are a great way to connect with a wider audience, there is no substitute for personalized, one-on-one communication. In a perfect world, the hiring partner at your firm would call up the dean at your biggest feeder school. She would let him know that proof of legal technology competence is now considered on par with membership on the Law Review for hiring purposes.[13] Assuming this a stretch, consider connecting with your counterpart at a feeder school to discuss current offerings and potential partnerships. If you manage library services, call up the director of the library. If you oversee legal project management or are the point person for e-discovery, consider contacting the head of experiential learning or the director of the clinical programs. One example where this could be effective is in cybersecurity. With recent high-profile hacks on large law firms, it would be ideal to inculcate proper cyber-hygiene in our students during law school. Without a real understanding of how cybersecurity works at the law firm level, however, it can be difficult for law schools to disseminate this information in a meaningful way. A conversation between the firm's head of IT and the library's IT point person could be a very interesting and ultimately fruitful partnership. Ultimately, this is all about starting a line of communication between the firm and those responsible for educating your future lawyers.

Conclusion

In what I am sure is a long list of priorities, getting involved in legal education is most likely not on yours. However, I hope this chapter gives you some incentive to add it there. I do not think it is hyperbolic to say that the continued existence of Big Law depends on recruiting technology-competent lawyers. While I know that changing law firm culture in and of itself is a struggle, firms are consistently innovating and doing more with less. Each new class of associates is an opportunity to move towards a more nimble and creative legal practice. This will happen much more quickly and efficiently if these new associates come in with an existing framework and background to meaningfully contribute to that cultural change. I encourage you to a be a part of making this the norm rather than the exception.

References

1. This chapter focuses on the issue of readying students for working in large law firms. The issues are different for students heading to smaller law firms or government/public interest positions.
2. Walter, K., "MoFo University Helps New Attorneys Bridge the Gap between Law School & Practice", Thomson Reuters Legal Executive Institute (June 16, 2017). See: http://www.legalexecutiveinstitute.com/law-school-survey-mofo-university/
3. Cohen, M. "Who Will Train Tomorrow's Lawyers and How Will They Learn?", *Forbes Magazine* (September 25, 2017). See: https://www.forbes.com/sites/markcohen1/2017/09/25/who-will-train-tomorrows-lawyers-and-how-will-they-learn/#69d24e317081

4. There is also an issue of scare resources within the law school. Changing curriculums require time and money, two resources rarely abundant within most law schools, particularly in these post-recession years.
5. Berger, T. "Three Generations and Two Tiers: How Participation in Law School Clinics and the Demand for 'Practice-Ready' Graduates Will Impact the Faculty Status of Clinical Law Professors", *Washington University Journal of Law and Politics* (2014). See: https://openscholarship.wustl.edu/cgi/viewcontent.cgi?article=1785&context=law_journal_law_policy
6. Grady, K. "What Teaching 'Legal-Tech' Could Mean", Medium Corporation (May 1, 2018). See: https://medium.com/the-algorithmic-society/what-teaching-legal-tech-could-mean-bf31cf0d4d10
7. See: https://www.legaltechinnovation.com/; updated as of October 31, 2017.
8. Walter, K., "Law School Case Study: U of Oklahoma Immerses Law Students in Technology", Thomson Reuters Legal Executive Institute (February 3, 2017). See: http://www.legalexecutiveinstitute.com/law-school-case-study-university-oklahoma-law/
9. This is a key component of the program and illustrates the support that the Digital Initiative has from the administration.
10. One interesting tool for teaching Microsoft Office products is Casey Flaherty's Procertas. While not a perfect program, participants are exposed to realistic legal tasks and trained on how to use Word, Excel, and Adobe efficiently. See: https://www.procertas.com/
11. Ward, S. "What's an inexpensive way to teach tech? Find outside experts, say law school librarians", *ABA Journal* (March 9, 2018). See: http://www.abajournal.com/news/article/whats_an_inexpensive_way_to_teach_tech_find_outside_experts_say_law_school/
12. Joseph Raczynski from Thomson Reuters guest spoke in my Legal Practice Technology course this past spring on the topic of Blockchain in the Law and was excellent at explaining this topic without focusing too much on any specific product.
13. The law firm Reed Smith recently announced that five out of their 60 incoming associates would be "summer technology associates." This is very interesting and, if more firms follow suit, could be a major wakeup call for the administration. Tashea, J. "Reed Smith launches legal tech summer associate program," *ABA Journal* (April 23, 2018). See: http://www.abajournal.com/news/article/reed_smith_launches_legal_tech_summer_associate_program

Chapter 6: Are you running a 24-hour law library?

By Jim Haggerty, vice president of LAC Group

Regardless of size, most law firms today see a growing volume of requests from practice groups asking for research related to topics such as M&A, intellectual property and franchising. Accompany these requests are additional inquiries for competitive intelligence (CI) and business intelligence (BI), which stem, in part, from partners mandating that attorneys shoulder more responsibility for finding new clients.

Facing an increasingly complex set of requests

One library manager from a mid-size Midwest law firm interviewed for this book noted: "there's no way [attorneys] have the time or tools for CI, and a lot of law firms don't have a separate researcher for CI". In spite of this, firm management is often reticent to hire full-time, non-attorney employees to tackle CI, research related to business development, or other areas of increased demand.

Jamie Blomquist, CIO for Maslon LLP – a mid-size law firm employing approximately 100 attorneys – says: "Attorneys are almost universally competent with research tools, such as Westlaw, but they're pressed for time and need data for business development". He adds that, "I want our library to be the place attorneys turn to if they're stuck, or even spending more than five minutes trying to start their research".

According to library managers, CI is a relatively new area of legal research and a hot topic for associations (e.g. AALL, SLA and LMA) with an interest in legal research. In fact, the LMA and Bloomberg Law recently published a joint survey stating that 62 percent of respondents say their "firm is increasing its emphasis/focus on business development and marketing efforts." Compared to a similar survey from just a few years ago, the 2018 LMA-Bloomberg Law research shows "a significant increase in the number of attorneys relying on business development professionals to complete… competitive intelligence tasks."

In the last year, law firm libraries have seen an increase in the time it takes to turn around CI and BI requests. For a large law firm with several hundred attorneys, these requests can reach (and often exceed) 10,000 queries per year. Library directors say there is ongoing pressure by firm management to reduce headcount in libraries, or to simply not replace librarians who retire or leave for other reasons. This dynamic causes experienced law library managers to struggle to find the right mix of after-hours coverage to handle a firm's needs and those of its clients.

According to one Midwest library manager at an Am Law 200 firm, attorneys increasingly fire off requests to her over the weekend looking for research support, but she holds all but the most urgent for fear her team will fall into a pattern in which they never truly step away from the work and recharge. Disconnecting from the work, she says, if even for a day, helps a researcher or any professional reset and actually improve productivity.

John DiGilio, senior director of Research & Intelligence for LibSource, part of LAC Group, concurs. DiGilio – who earned his MA in library and information services, along with a JD degree – has worked for large and mid-size law firms and legal information vendors such as Thomson Reuters for more than 20 years. He remembers working at law firms as the library director when management would ask him to staff the law library for after-hours work.

"I participated in pilots, coming in on a Saturday or Sunday to figure out if people were using the law library's services," recalls DiGilo. "The decision to staff and how to staff often stemmed from anecdotes; management would hear from an attorney about wanting to have service on weekends or holidays, and we would soon be scrambling to respond."

Each time DiGilio took part in after-hours projects, he never recalls getting four straight hours of work to fill his time. Ultimately, he says, the firms would say it cost too much to have him waiting for requests.

"With research services, it's not easy for firms to get a grasp on how much after-hours research service they'd use if they had it available," adds DiGilio. "Many firms operate as an island, and they look at having to pay someone to be available, almost on stand-by, to manage an expectation."

During his time at Reed Smith LLP, DiGilio saw the firm offer late-night work processed via paralegals because management saw that offering as a necessity, and it was clear attorneys tapped into the services regularly. DiGilio believes a recipe of equal parts technology and staffing can make more complicated research and retrieval efficient and measurable, which proves the strategic worth of both.

Putting in place strategies to keep up

Many of today's library managers are looking to transform their services, better manage the volume of requests, and measure these queries and responses. A library director at a West Coast law firm with two hundred attorneys on staff says he's seeing anywhere from 40 to 70 research requests per day ranging from business development inquiries to legislative history.

One industry observer and practitioner that has seen and written about nearly every facet of library and knowledge science is Jean O'Grady, who is an author, research professional, and blogger at Dewey B Strategic. With her law degree, 30-year career as a research director and an MA in library science, O'Grady speaks and opines on the technology and strategies librarians need to know about.

"Attorneys shouldn't be doing CI; that's squarely on the shoulders of the law library," says O'Grady. "That's one of the multiple, important areas that now should reside with the firm's information and content expert: the librarian."

O'Grady expresses concern for any librarians who might still be reluctant to take on the processing of the quantities of information to deliver a superior response to CI queries. In that vacuum, law firm management might tap other departments, such as paralegals or IT, where the staff lack business resource and curated search expertise.

"Being a librarian is a form of knowledge management. Unfortunately there was a trend to treat KM as a technology problem that could be solved through the implementation of a piece of software," remarks O'Grady. "KM projects designed without the expertise of research and knowledge professionals have given KM a bad name."

Recent surveys of both law firm leaders and clients (e.g., Altman and Weil) indicate that KM is now viewed as a key strategy for driving efficient lawyer workflow. Law librarians are emerging as leaders of this second wave of KM.

"Not only are they familiar with the work product created by both transactional lawyers and litigators, but they also know how to marry internal content and internal business intelligence with commercial sources of analytics and business intelligence," adds O'Grady. "This combination of knowledge assets can drive custom insights through the organization."

O'Grady recalls creating a KM database for her firm in 1986, but KM was never solely a technology for her. Instead, she sees the practice of KM as understanding the lawyer's workflow and the importance of combining indexing and free text. Librarians are incredibly skilled in this way, she believes, and they know what makes a good KM process and product.

Taking that skill and translating it into analytics and algorithms, combined with data, is something DiGilio and O'Grady see as an opportunity for law libraries and librarians. These services – along with creating self-service widgets and tools can help the library reduce the time for document retrieval – so researchers can focus on more complex activities. Automating low-level activities helps to meet the pressing volume of complex requests as staffing becomes tighter.

"We have an inconsistent volume of work," says the West Coast library director referenced earlier. "Hiring an overflow service to manage the spikes was better than committing to hiring another FTE who might not stay busy."

DiGilio says a firm may find it cost prohibitive to have a full-time staffer dedicated to research, CI and BI, especially when firms look at the bottom line and cut costs. One way around this is to have several firms come together, hire a third party and pay only for what research services they use. This approach, say some firms who are employing DiGilio's suggestion, is economical because librarians are not paying an employee for an eight-hour day on a Saturday; rather, the third party bills the firm only for the 1.45 hours of research carried out for any one law library, for example.

"The third-party model leverages its ability to meet the workload with a service at an affordable rate," says DiGilio.

The model alone isn't the only consideration. It's critical to look at how a provider is staffing its model. Any viable service provider ought to have people on board who have the relevant credentials and proven research skills a law librarian would hire as a full-time employee. If a law firm isn't in a position to pay one of its researchers the necessary overtime to handle after-hours staffing, then DiGilio sees a third-party partnership as workable solution.

Another possible way to reduce the library's workload – although not roundly advocated for – is partnering with a local university to recruit a student in an MLIS program who would handle lower level tasks. This, in turn, frees up experienced librarians to handle CI or BI work. One concern with partnering with an MLIS program is this: unless the MLIS student has a law degree, they've likely never handled legal research, so there's a possibly steep learning curve to climb to be effective. If a firm's librarian were to bring in a student to assist with the library's workload, protecting client confidentiality would also be a necessary consideration.

As for other options law firms might consider to keep up with mushrooming requests, none of the law firms we interviewed believe it's feasible to have newly hired attorneys reply to research requests, in effect pinch-hitting for the law library research team. With starting salaries for attorneys hovering around $200,000 annually, firms want their young attorneys focused on billable work.

Reflecting on the future and past

When asked to project themselves forward in time, envisioning a fully automated library with a storehouse of all-digital assets at the ready, librarians saw a role for artificial intelligence (AI). However, many felt that even working with bots would require an attorney to ask pointed questions that often only a research expert would know how to posit in order to synthesize information.

Librarians and attorneys with more than 20 years of experience working in and alongside law libraries recall living through the explosion of information served up by WestLaw, Lexis and even the internet. Initially, WestLaw and Lexis required special terminals. The software then became available on attorneys' computers. Eventually, the internet was felt to be the harbinger of the end times for librarians and professional research staff. With each technological development, pundits and vendors heralded a cure-all of self-serve research.

However, a system is only as good as the person approaching it. Similarly to the technologies before, AI portends a new level of complexity for attorneys and researchers to grapple with.

"I taught classes on how to use internet search engines to do legal research; everything we worried about in terms of getting bad information from search-engine queries was also a concern in one way or another with research before the internet was born," recalls DiGilio. "Every technological advance was supposed to make it easier for the attorney. But I've never been in a library and seen the workload go down."

Advice for the pros from the pros

Law firms are knowledge organizations, yet most law firms don't put their librarian in the C-suite. It's remarkable that IT and marketing professionals have a seat at most firms' executive table and librarians don't, especially when the latter have been a part of the law firm fabric decades before the other professional disciplines arrived.

"If the information professional doesn't have a seat, they then can't give guidance on solving problems," adds O'Grady. "Librarians have to influence information policy, so they have to lobby for access."

Taking ownership of CI and BI may just be the way for librarians to finally get that seat. Embracing the workload and adding technology and outside partnerships tackles the tactical challenge of meeting a 24/7 demand. Librarians who have taken the steps to transform their operation to become truly 24/7 operations have also seen management's perception of them shift from tactical role player to a strategic partner.

Chapter 7: How strong relationships and expertise aid business development with clients – a case study

By Cynthia Brown, director of research services at Littler Mendelson PC, and Jill L Kilgore, research librarian at Littler Mendelson PC

The project finds its way to the library

Most opportunities have a simple beginning: the big ideas come from identifying a need and boldly pursuing the options. This story begins with a client who had a need: in-house council could not field the number of calls they were receiving daily. The calls from human resource professionals were valid and required legal advice, but the legal department was being overwhelmed. In addition to simply responding to question at hand, the client wanted to understand the types of calls they were receiving and what information was sent out to the business units. They needed help providing the advice, but they also wanted to capture the types of questions asked and any subsequent data created through the process. This client started by approaching their shareholder, who knew to reach out to the knowledge management department, whose chief knowledge officer saw a role for the library. The legal services portion of the project was arranged in a traditional format by the attorneys answering client phone calls and providing advice, but a system was needed to gather, organize, and synthesize the information shared between the client and attorneys. Utilizing existing technology, the library developed a tracking system for each call and a means of categorizing the resulting data. The library saw an opportunity to utilize unique librarian proficiencies and enrich the final work product provided to the client. This case study will show the reader the evolution of the project and how the library identified the need and initiated the pursuit.

Tailoring a project solution

After the shareholder was connected to the library, a tool needed to be designed. While the existing technology had been in use by the library and knowledge management departments to gather and organize information used to produce reports, this client-facing project was unique and required a tailored solution. The library facilitated a collaboration of an IT department, project shareholder and attorneys, and the client to produce a flexible system.

While the library would maintain and manage the gathering and organization of information, they would not be entering it for the attorneys. The shareholder leading the project wanted the attorneys to be able to enter their information from an incoming call and resulting advice quickly and simply; therefore, before the team of attorneys could begin tracking their advice, they needed training in order to use the system. Without accurate and consistent data entries, the reports would be of little use to the client.

Initially an inventory was taken by interviewing the stakeholders to determine what information would be expected in the final reports. The library created a taxonomy, determined data entry fields, and fashioned draft reports using feedback from the reference interview. The design was focused on the desired result. Stakeholders were queried: what did they want to know, and what conclusions were they looking to draw from the reports? Understanding, for instance, that it was important for the head of the legal department to be able to review if there were large number of termination conversations coming out of one business unit helped to create the required data fields to gather and report on that particular issue. The reports were then reverse-engineered to the specifications desired for the end results.

The users put it to the test

The attorneys were new users to the system, so the library began by establishing individual access. Like all new users, the attorneys came to the project with varying levels of technical experience and familiarity. To ensure comfort for each attorney, the library offered group trainings and individual sessions as needed. These sessions also offered an opportunity to test user experience and modify the interface based on the anticipated and resulting functionality and usability. After the tool underwent a few iterations, the team arranged a demonstration for the client. Each business unit from the client was represented as well as the original stakeholders. The library took the lead in the meeting, showing a step-by-step approach to using the system. The client was able to see the project from the incoming phone call to the data entry, categorization, reporting functionality, and resulting analytics provided for future business decisions. Taking the comments and suggestions from this meeting, the library made further revisions to the tool and overall process to enhance the product. With approval from the client, the hotline and reporting were ready to launch.

As the project came to life, the library was instrumental in facilitating changes and answering questions about the tool. Improvements organically grew out of the process as attorneys were trained and began using the new solution. Sample reports were created initially as examples of the possible visualizations and production of the data. The reports were then fine-tuned until the client was satisfied with the information. Once the attorneys entered calls into the system, a date was determined for the first reports. After a few iterations, production of the reports began in earnest and were distributed to the client weekly. Once a statistically significant amount of data had been gathered, the library team evaluated the reports for trends or necessary changes to the taxonomy. While generating the data visualizations, patterns formed and additions were made to the reported fields. The attorney-client communications were documented with increasing granularity, capturing more information while maintaining the flexibility required from the client. Based on generated feedback, the project has been a success with the stakeholders reporting tremendous praise, and the library is now looking for additional opportunities to offer these types of services to the firm and firm clients.

Learning from a case study

In reviewing the case study, one could logically ask: what makes this success different from any other project involving the library? Hotlines run through a firm have had varying success in the industry. Tales of lost time and little profits are heard from the law firm side, and reports of inaction or receiving little more than phone calls are murmured from the client side. This hotline was something different. It expanded into a results-oriented product with reporting features and visualizations. The client was able to do more than answer one question at a time or fix a single issue before moving on to the next. This project included opportunities for the client to implement changes and solutions as a direct result of the library's involvement.

In this instance, the client had work in-house that they were willing to give to the firm. In-house council did not have the bandwidth to field the calls, and they had little to no ability to synthesize the data produced in each call. The reputation of the library gave an opportunity to enhance a run-of-the-mill hotline offering. Neither the client nor the shareholder knew what would be required or what the library could offer. The library saw a need and presented a greater product for the client as a result. This proactive approach demonstrates how libraries can play an active role in capturing client work. Not all client needs can be solved by an attorney acting alone. The technology, the skills, and the taxonomy existed in the library's toolbox before the client's need. When the opportunity presented itself, the library was therefore poised and ready to act. The data curation and resulting reporting was more than the client could do on their own and highlighted offerings from the library. Connecting the library and clients is the next natural evolution of legal services. This case study demonstrates the value a library can provide given the opportunity; however, in this situation, things were in place and the team was ready when the interdepartmental opportunity presented itself.

Connecting librarian skills to client needs

With this opportunity, the library drew on its vast research capabilities and resources to produce a client-centered solution. The team facilitated the development of an effective and flexible taxonomy. Firstly, applying the inherent skills of the librarian produced clean and categorized data, which was then gathered, organized, and manipulated to provide a synthesis of quantitative and qualitative outputs. The reports are only as good as the data, so having a librarian present and collaborating during the entire process ensured consistency in the taxonomy and the data. While the work performed by the attorneys is helpful in the present, the reports created are capable of generating long-term change for the client, who can take direct action with business decisions following the results of the data analytics. Not only can they review the details of the calls, but the data visualizations also allow for a quick snapshot of trends and display information that is easily digestible in an increasingly busy world. By involving the library, not only does the client receive a better result, but the library is also given new opportunities to apply their professional abilities.

One could ask: does this project simply create an administrative position for the library, or is this a real opportunity for in-depth analysis? While all projects have elements of administrative work, these reports require the expertise of an information professional to regularly review reports and trends, and analyze and improve the taxonomy as needed. Data visualizations present large and oftentimes complex sets of data in easily comprehensible graphics. They are appealing and increasingly a client expectation; however, the analysis behind the data visualization is the gem that the library offers. This service allows the client to draw conclusions, identify areas of concern, and implement solutions/take direct business action. The client takes the reports and applies them to their business needs, allowing them to resolve issues promptly. No other department in a law firm is poised to provide this type of work to a client. Libraries need to look for opportunities where solutions begin and necessitate continued maintenance in their department. Making the library the most attractive option will ensure its continued growth and prominence.

The next step: find another need

This case study demonstrates that libraries can and should do this type of data analysis and visualization work. The overlapping skills present in libraries are a hallmark of the library world. Libraries can see a project from its infancy to its launch and then, most importantly, can continue to modify the system by monitoring trends and improving the taxonomy as it inevitably evolves. Without a group maintaining a system like this, the reports would be increasingly less useful to the client.

There has been much discussion of the term "analytics" recently; in fact, some may say the term has become a buzzword used for marketing purposes, losing much of its value. The term can be changed, but the results are the same. In this case study, librarians collected, sorted, stored, and retrieved critical information. The information retrieved is enhanced because of how the original data was collected, sorted, and stored. The critical analysis of the data creates the outputs, allowing the client to make informed decisions. The project moves then from simply freeing up in-house council's time to a resource where all incoming questions from HR are stored. This was not simply data visualization but an end-to-end solution beyond the capabilities of the in-house counsel and project attorneys. Meshing the skills of the attorneys with the library provided the synergy to create something special.

These results-oriented products provided by a law firm to a client fit the bill for a post-recession legal world. Clients need more, and librarians can offer these services to the forward-thinking law firm and law library. It is important to note that a non-proactive library would not be ready for or even considered for such an opportunity. To take part in such a project requires good relationships, excellent reputation, innovative thinking, and the ability to utilize fundamental skills of librarianship in a new application.

Chapter 8: The evolution of a law library from physical to mobile

By CJ Anderson, head of information and research at Linklaters LLP, London

Introduction

In 2013, in response to lawyer feedback, the Linklaters London Information & Research Center was created by merging the collections and staff from 13 practice-based libraries. This brought London in line with Linklaters offices in the rest of the world by providing a central library to support the whole office (legal and business teams) with legal and business information and research services. This merger was achieved over two years by a series of "mini-mergers", initially into three locations and finally into a prime location, to maximize footfall, located next to the staff restaurant and IT service desk.

Five years ago, when we started our transformation journey, the collection occupied 517 square meters and had 1,490 meters of shelf space (with additional growth room). This calculation didn't include office space for most of the staff, who sat in their own office separate from their practice collection.

Each merger reduced the amount of space available to us, and being in a prime high-footfall area of the building has meant that in the last three years our physical location has reduced twice more in response to the changing needs of the firm to accommodate IT support and an Innovation Lab in this area of the building.

Today, the London Information & Research Center occupies 60 square meters of space and 30 meters of shelf space. There is an archival storage space for materials in the basement for a further 50 meters of our collection, and 20 meters remain in the corridors around the building for local use by lawyers. The team sit with the rest of the knowledge and learning team in an open plan office, seven floors away from the Information & Research Center, and move between this space, the enquiry desk in the Information & Research Center, and hot-desks in practice locations as required.

Despite the reduction in space, the team and the services they provide are still as highly used and as valued as they were when the process of shrinking started. The team and the resources are no less visible and are, in some cases, being used more. Most of our services and interactions are online. How did we get from there to here?

Drivers for and direction of change

Even at the point we reacted to internal demand by centralizing the information and research service for the office, we recognized that there were several other factors which would impact the future of the global information and research team and the services they provide. While we started by streamlining our physical space, we knew that we would have to look at how we supported the firm and the services we provided; however, during the early stages I don't think any of us would have predicted how all-encompassing the move to mobile would be.

In 2013, the UK economy started to show signs of recovery after one of the longest periods of economic stagnation on record. Real GDP was still way below the 2008 peak and the UK economy grew by 1.9 percent, which was its strongest rate since 2007 but was still below its pre-recession peak; growth was also slowing.[1] This seemed like a dark time, as actual or potential recession impacted every country and previously sound companies failed. With the effects of the financial crisis still being felt, most organizations took a cautious approach to budgeting, with several library services reporting that while there was pressure to review and reduce content budgets, they remained stable. The services themselves, however, were experiencing mixed fortunes, with law firms struggling.[2]

For corporate and law firm libraries, this led to questions being asked about the ability of conventional information and research services to survive changed user demands, disruptive technologies, the value being added by professional information staff, and the impacts of the ever-increasing pressure on costs and central overheads. These profession-wide questions gave us a framework (which we used then and still use today) to explore and articulate the drivers for change and to help shape our responses to them.

1. Changed user demands

The business of law

There have been (and continue to be) changes in the practice of law itself. Pressure from clients and therefore competition in the legal profession to provide outstanding legal services for lower prices is changing the way law firms do business. Many law firms are looking at different billing methods and, in some cases, moving away from the billable hour as they focus more attention on customer service while at the same time looking for internal efficiencies in how they provide those services. This means more commoditized services and delivering the same work with fewer people or different mixes of seniority, skill and profession.

For a law library, this means not just supporting lawyers and marketing/business development staff, but also supporting paralegals, legal project managers, legal technologists and business managers, so that everyone working for the firm has the same access to and support for the information & research services they need to do their job effectively.

The generation gap

In 2014, the UK Commission for Employment and Skills published a report which summarized their research exploring the future of work and how jobs, and the skills needed in the workplace, would change by 2030. It suggested that computer algorithms would replace professionals in many areas (including law) and that an aging population would create four-generation offices where staff in their seventies would work alongside those in their twenties.

Library services are now supporting users who range from those who grew up with paper to so-called digital natives, who probably didn't even have a school library and are used to doing everything online (and without email). The diversity of competence in internet and/or electronic based searching cannot be assumed to split neatly along generational lines.

There was, and continues to be, demand for better and different access to information sources and services, which is a direct result of changes to the academic library experience – for example, more distance learning courses, the ubiquitous nature of access to online legal information, social networking, mobile devices, and electronic textbooks. Each new generation of lawyers expects much more from their information and research service than a physical, face-to-face interaction within a library.

The agile, flexible workforce

The combined impacts of changes to the business of law and a multi-generational workforce means that we now must support a population of agile workers who are used to flexible working.[3]

This agility is important for organizations to redesign jobs around AI, robotics and new business models, which has led to the reshaping (and perhaps ultimately the scrapping) of the up or out career ladder. If an individual is to succeed in having a 70-year career, they must be able to change directions throughout this journey to align with evolving roles.

Instead of staff (including lawyers) who have a steady progression along a linear job-based pathway which takes them from trainee to director/partner, we now support individuals who are empowered and encouraged to acquire valuable experiences and explore new roles. In practical terms, we are having to think about how easy it is for users to find services and resources in areas they don't know – for example, a lawyer moving to another practice or staying with their practice and moving to another office. A side-benefit is that because these people are empowered to manage their own development and actively encouraged to engage with learning opportunities, getting their attention and engagement with training provided by the Information & Research Center has become easier.

Flexibility, or a flexible workforce, historically meant the ability that firms had to adapt to changing workforce demands by scaling the number of staff up (or down) quickly in areas where they were unable to commit to full-time, permanent positions. This was most commonly seen in the alternative resourcing space with contract-based paralegals. Over the last few years this definition has expanded to encompass an individual's ability to control when, how and where they work to achieve the work/life balance that suits them best. Organizationally this is done through a combination of formal policies which are often struggling to keep up with the pace of change/current demands and informal policies where individual line managers support a model that works for both the team and the individual involved. These informal policies are often the pilot or prototypes that ultimately become the formal policies.

For the individual this means control over things like start and end times, days and hours worked, and the location in which the work is done. For the information and research service, this means that there is an expectation from their user base (and therefore an expectation within the I&R service strategy) that everything should be available from everywhere.

2. Disruptive technologies

Thanks to the great thinking already completed and published, a picture of a potential future for law firms started to emerge. It became apparent that increasing innovation in this space means that we are moving from a time where products driven by large corporations are the only ones available to a time where anyone with a way to make things simpler and smarter can succeed. Internal discussions on strategy at a senior level in our firm were based around this potential future; these culminated in the creation of an innovation and efficiency team which the information and research service could engage with to clarify the impact, involvement and expectations of new legal technologies and teams on the information professionals and their services.

In parallel, for the same reasons the information and research service was looking at the impact of changing user demands, the firm's IT department was doing its own review and outlining a program to achieve a seamless workplace transition on a global scale and deliver a step change in the user experience, enabling Linklaters to better service its clients. The first of these changes was to equip users worldwide with Windows 10 technology and replace desktops (for all lawyers and for business teams by need) with laptops or tablets. The second change was to replace Blackberrys with smartphones and enable access to emails and some other content on personal smartphones. This resulted in an increase in the firm's expectations that global information and research teams would be able to provide everything, everywhere – and on three operating systems (Windows 10, iOS, Android).

3. The value being added by professional information staff and their services

The clearly articulated idea that technology would transform the whole business of law, combined with the ubiquitous nature of Google, led to senior management thinking about the future value of information and research services to the firm. A natural question was whether a smaller role (and team) was to be the way forward.

This conflicted with the increasing demand from junior lawyers and from across business teams for improved services. Users were pushing for a high quality, responsive research service which made it easier to get support for complex legal and business enquiries. The development of a new tactical opportunities team highlighted the need for an expanded competitive intelligence capability which could focus on defining, gathering, analyzing and distributing intelligence about products, clients, sectors, markets and countries to support decision making. Users also wanted better access to self-service tools and more support in using them effectively.

The problems that lawyers had in finding and using the right information online remained similar to those which existed in the physical world. The digital world just exponentially increased the sheer volume of information available to users, which made it difficult to sort the useful from the unhelpful; harder to identify the quality and reliability of information (too much fake news); challenging to identify the specific information in the form in which lawyers need it; and apparent that the nature of information was (and still is) changing.

It was clear that the purpose of a law library and its value to the organization remained the same, but how services were made available and the proportion of information staff time devoted to each service would need to change. The fundamental principles that the availability of information and professional information staff enables the firm to maintain are: the quality of its services to clients; the avoidance of mistakes due to a lack of information; and the support of the development and maintenance of client relationships. These could be carried into our new digital, flexible, mobile environment.

4. Pressure on costs and central overheads

The two areas of costs which specifically impact law libraries (or information and research functions) are market driven and difficult for a law firm to control: premises and information resources.

The cost of rent in most major cities is increasing, with the average cost per square meter in the City of London being around £70.[4] The number of people who work for firms is increasing but the office space leased by firms is staying the same or decreasing. This is possible due to open plan offices and mobile computing (laptops and tablets) so supporting efforts to reduce pressure on premises cost are already, to an extent, factored into plans to support a flexible workforce. Premises managers who are looking to squeeze more people into existing office space often see the physical library as an easy target, especially when services and resources are online. It is difficult to challenge that assumption and articulate the value of a library space in a way that speaks to the bottom line in the same way as more desks for fee-earners does.

All information and research service budgets are under ongoing pressure due to significant increases in the cost of information resources and diminishing annual budgetary increases or even outright cuts.[5] Having adequate digital collections particularly incurs significant costs, as you can't rely on having a copy of a book on a shelf which can be borrowed by anyone who needs it but must have a license to a digital copy to ensure that anyone can use it whether they are in or out of the office. It is a fallacy that trimming down the number of books and journals in a law library to make physical space creates a saving, as it does not necessarily offset the increased costs digital resources command.

Getting to everything, everywhere

What became apparent as we were going through our evaluation stage is that the legal sector is in a state of change and that change was going to be the only constant for both the firm and for our information and research services. Everything about where and how the team worked and the services they provided to lawyers was going to have to change.

We identified immediate challenges from the requirement to downsize the library space, budgetary constraints, rapidly changing technology, and the need to manage stakeholder expectations. Despite the downsizing and cost control, we had significant opportunities available to us in providing better services and access to information; increasing our collaboration and engagement with the business; developing self-sufficient end users; and creating sustainable practices and operations to act as a foundation for further change. The question was: how were we going to do it?

To quote Creighton Abrams, "when eating an elephant take one bite at a time".[6] We needed to divide the needs and the work required to fulfil those needs into bite-sized pieces and work with our users to facilitate innovation through incremental change.[7] The drivers for change became apparent at different times in our change journey, which helped us to identify the right issue to address at each stage and the stories which we would need to share with our users to help them be comfortable with the changes we were making.

We firstly focused on the areas of change which had immediate drivers and mapped them onto our six areas of service provision. Following consultation with lawyers and other users, these were further divided into two categories: those which our users could identify as being visible and important to support them, and those that were more "back office" activities which we knew people would notice if they weren't being done.

Mostly "invisible" to our users			Highly visible to our users		
Library management	Information procurement	Information asset management	Research and enquiry services	Current awareness	End user training

Our second area of focus was to identify the opportunities that could come out of each of the areas of change. Since flexible (mobile) working was emerging as the biggest driver, we invested time to work with our IT colleagues to understand the art of the possible in each space. We took a short, medium and long-term view of each of the technology opportunities to phase our approach to change, so that we could deliver realistic, incremental and achievable innovation which wouldn't be wasted effort as time and technology moved on.

It is a universally accepted truth that busy lawyers who are (rightly) focused on clients only pay attention to what's going on inside the firm when there is a burning platform driving change or they are confronted with a change that appears to make them lose something they are accustomed to. Our third action was to combine our timeline of burning platforms and opportunities with storytelling about what could be lost if we didn't change and how much better it would be if we did do something new to craft a compelling narrative. These stories were used to firstly get the information and research team in agreement, followed by senior management and then legal and business teams.

We articulated this strategy as "Everything, Everywhere"; it had four distinct work streams, overseen the global information and research leadership team. I should probably add at this point that the changes within each workstream were made by global working groups of information and research team members who added these projects to their normal day jobs so that service to and support for the firm wasn't disrupted – even during periods of library downsizing.

Collection management

With space previously not being an issue, the separate London collections had not been through a formal office-wide review process for many years. Faced with the need to significantly reduce the size of the collection we had to quickly devise a simple set of actions which could reduce our holdings.

Weeding

In the initial project, which lasted six months, the information advisors met for weekly meetings initially to brainstorm and agree actions and then to feedback on progress and agree next steps. They initially divided the collection into books (including standing orders), loose-leafs and journals. For each of these categories, they identified the materials which we had available online already and gathered usage metrics. This was used as the basis to propose to practice support lawyers (PSLs) and knowledge and learning (K&L) partners that we get rid of hardcopies altogether where the online version is heavily used. This allowed stakeholders to challenge our assumption; they pushed back on only those titles which they felt had most value in hardcopy. The lists were prepared from the library management system (LMS) and were the formal titles, not the commonly used titles, so discussions with PSLs and K&L Partners also included a "show and tell" element where information advisors were able to point to an item on the shelf or on a trolley they brought with them to highlight exactly which title was under discussion.

In parallel, based on usage (both observed and recorded in the LMS), information advisors were discussing and agreeing how many copies of duplicated titles we need. Some items (like the Oxford English Dictionary) were held in every library and often in multiple copies. To demonstrate the challenge, we created a central space where examples of multiple duplicates could be lined up on a shelf. This list of titles and the proposed numbers to be kept was shared and discussed with PSLs and K&L partners.

Subsequent projects targeted moving more paper-only journal subscriptions to electronic only and agreeing a cut-off date (in 2017, we used 2005 as the cut-off date) to identify another tranche of books for disposal. Since we had a challenging experience getting users to review lists in the early project and had more success when showing the titles being discussed, the books for disposal were moved together into a "review shelf" (which was nearly nine shelves full in the end); PSLs were invited to browse these and remove anything they wanted to be kept. We allowed two weeks for PSL review, and under one shelf was retained.

Disposal

For recent titles we looked for book charities or other libraries that wanted the items we were disposing of. Everything else went into a recycling process. The manual labor element of scooping things off shelves into skips was divided between the whole team, as was updating the library management system (LMS) to delete the records associated with the items being disposed of.

There was also a category of titles which were identified as not needed on the main library shelves but needed in the building "just in case". This led to the expansion of our "archival" storage space in the basement to house four times the materials it was intended for. Again, items were manually moved and shelved downstairs and a new location of "Archived" created on the LMS so the records could be updated.

Policy

Finally, we had to update our retention policies to ensure that we actively managed these collections going forwards, as we didn't have the space to grow. These have been refreshed and updated every time the Information & Research Center space has been reduced and a collection review has taken place.

We also implemented an "information places" policy which explains to the global team what information about which products needed to be stored where. For example, an electronic subscription resource needs to be recorded in the LMS and on the intranet, both as an entry in the Research Source SharePoint list and as a Research Source wiki page.

Publicity and training

As we were going through these hardcopy collection reduction projects, we were making our users aware of what we were doing and how they could find the online resources. We used the office bulletin, local practice and business team blogs, meetings, drop-in sessions, publicity stands outside the staff restaurant, email updates and posters.

We also rebranded our online library catalogue as eLibrary; users can include it as one of the key apps on the home page of the intranet. It is also linked to from practice knowhow wiki pages, information and research team office pages, and anywhere else we can think of to keep it visible to users.

Intranet wiki pages were created for each research resource to explain what it is, how it can be accessed, what the licensing restrictions are, whether or not it is recharged or paid for centrally, how to get help (from information and research staff and/or directly from the vendor) and access to training materials (videos, eLearning, quick reference guides, etc). These were also linked to the LMS catalogue record.

The challenge of how to inform new joiners led to a separate global project to standardize training on knowledge and information tools. This piece of work led to the creation of a half-day new joiner session on this topic which is included in each office's new joiner induction. It is followed up by an email with links to the key places to look for these tools and an invite to a second training session about a month after joining.

Impact of mobile lawyers

Feedback, particularly from lawyers, was telling us that the LMS was difficult to use, and most lawyers weren't willing to use it at all. Discussions to find out why uncovered a view that it was too old fashioned in its design, so it was hard to immediately understand what they were looking at and impossible to use on a mobile. The next project replaced the old LMS with one that is mobile friendly, easy for lawyers to use, and adds functionality that we didn't have before (pictures of the book covers). We are continuing to roll-out new features as feedback (from lawyers and information and research team members) dictates.

The other piece of frequent feedback was that there were too many logins and passwords to remember, and for those titles that were accessed via IP authentication, the experience when working from outside the office was too slow. This is where conversations with our IT teams really intensified as we came up a steep learning curve to understand the new technology infrastructure and what was possible for us to leverage within it. We learned about alternative single sign-on capabilities (SAML/ADFS) and the IT strategy to move away from IP authentication.

Again, this led to the development of a separate (and ongoing) cross-functional project which started by canvassing our electronic journal and database vendors to establish which were ready to move away from IP authentication or to skip that stage altogether and move from login/password directly to SAML. When we started the answer was none, but in the last 12 months we have started to make progress – albeit slowly.

For many information and research teams the answer to excessive logins to remember is a browser-based, centrally managed password and metrics gathering system. At the time we started looking for a solution, no vendor could provide one which would work in all three of the browsers we needed to support. Our services need to be available via Microsoft Edge on desktop PCs, laptops and tablets, as well as via Safari and Chrome on mobile phones. This decision is constantly under review so that when the market changes, we can revisit our assumptions and conclusions.

Procurement and vendor management

By going mobile and moving to virtual rather than physical collections, we expanded our list of vendors, and in a central single team, information and research staff could share the load of vendor management. We devised a system whereby key vendor relationships would be managed by a senior manager (the vendor nominee) and individual titles within that vendor's portfolio would be looked after by a named information advisor (the title nominee). These individuals would work with the central information procurement team (part of the firm's sourcing and supply function) to articulate new requirements and share user feedback to inform renewal discussions and other meetings as required.

The role of the information procurement team expanded to include challenging nominees who try to add content which is already available on another source and ensuring that we have the right licenses in place for the legal and business teams to be able to use external information in the way they need to. The information professional's role in guiding purchasing decisions to enable the right tools to be available for self-service and complex legal and business research is expanded rather than diminished in the digital world, since online resources are so much more expensive than hard-copy titles.

The next area to consider is personal copies of eBooks; however, until there is a strong driver for change, this opportunity remains unexploited.

Other impacts

In addition to lawyers engaging with self-service and doing more research for themselves, our current awareness services were an area which required incremental changes as new technologies became available and as lawyer behavior moved from push only to a balance of push and pull. This was driven in part by the move to mobile and in part by the increased use of smart phones, which increased expectations of what is possible. Initially the changes were simple, such as having an email alert that was readable on a mobile phone and converting our Word template-based newsletters into intranet blogs. With more information being rolled up into topic pages on the intranet, we started to include information advisor managed RSS feeds as a content source. With more people receiving their emails on their phones, the volume of alerts generated by a one email per topic or per practice model is too high, so we are exploring one email per person and how we can help the user personalize that email for themselves.

Identity and brand

In 2013, the information and research service was defined by the physical spaces it maintained. These were called either libraries or information units depending on the office and were very clearly seen as the place to go to find information and research materials. The pressure on space (more lawyers to find desks for means less room for libraries) meant that even when a location for the new combined library was found, it would be significantly smaller. We wondered what the impact on relationship with users would be. If our identity as a team is separated from the physical space we occupied, how will our users know who we are and what value we have to offer? If we correctly articulate identity as "consistent, engaging artefacts", can we use that definition to tell our story and engage our users with us in a familiar and meaningful way? If brand is defined as the relationship between an organization and an audience, and the information and research team members aren't co-located with their users, how can we maintain the good relationships, high usage, and feedback that states we are a valuable part of the business?

An opportunity was identified when a new Microsoft SharePoint based firm-wide intranet[8] proved to be a success with users and attracted high usage numbers – something previous intranets had failed to do. We had been given the opportunity to have our "Research Sources" – a list of all our subscription based electronic databases and journals – in the top navigation of the new intranet; it was and remains consistently in the top five most used pages on the intranet. This was our platform to create a consistent set of wiki pages which articulated our services and resources and reflected our brand.

Once we had agreed on our identity as "information and research", we worked with the online content team (also part of the knowledge and learning function) to create three templates which could be used: (1) office-based information and research services; (2) legal and business information resources; and (3) services and non-office aligned teams. These templates were constructed so that we could achieve global consistency; however, there is still flexibility for local teams to reflect the needs of their users. These templates are referred to in our information places policy.

In our model of leveraging opportunities for incrementing change, our next improvement to these pages was to include roll-ups of relevant blog content and now that the intranet is available on mobile phones as well as laptops and tablets, we're working on making the pages less wordy and more icon based for navigating page content.

Impact on the people in our team

In maintaining the team's identity and brand, the team has made efforts to regularly hot-desk, to walk the floors and to attend practice group meetings and training sessions so that they remain a visible and named point of contact for the practices they support. Meetings with PSLs, K&L partners, and marketing teams are more formal and diarized regularly. They are spending time with business managers to understand each practice group's business plan and to make sure that they are invited to be involved in practice initiatives where their skills and expertise can add value.

The changes from physical to mobile have let our information professionals utilize their skills in new and different ways as experimenters and drivers of change. They have always been cataloguers, researchers, current awareness providers, abstracters and trainers – we still must help our users find, store and explore the information we buy for them. They have an increased role as market analysts and prospectors – supporting business development efforts and working to help mine data (both internally and externally) to help make sense of the world we operate in by helping users understand what data is available to them and how best to use it.

We have had to add new skills to their repertoire like eLearning designers, relationship managers (with vendors as well as legal and business teams), project managers, content creators and providers of decision ready information.

There are also new opportunities where information professionals have the power to influence the internal landscape and the changing legal publishing industry. They can help drive the media in which information is published and can drive or defeat efforts to increase open-source publishing and open access to legal information.

Conclusion

So what does a mobile information and research service mean? In the beginning, it looked like a simple collection management issue of moving from a physical library to online, but over the course of five years it has impacted all our services and all our people. We have delivered projects about global standard lawyer training, the technology we use to login to services, an upgraded library catalogue, standard wiki page templates and the content within them, an improved procurement and vendor management methodology, new current awareness services, and decision ready research. We have learned that nothing is a simple as it seems, and that change doesn't stop. The checklist for success in moving from physical to mobile is much like that of any other project:

- Identify the drivers for change;
- Identify opportunities to improve or replace or do something new;
- Craft the narrative (the stories) which will support your case for change;

- Make your resources visible and support people to use them;
- Review your services and consider what you can stop doing to make room for what you want to start doing;
- Identify opportunities for incremental improvements or innovations;
- Articulate your identity and brand and give it equal attention to everything else; and
- Don't forget the impact that change has on people – help your team and your users get ready for change.

References

1. BBC News. (2014). *UK economy growing at fastest rate since 2007.* BBC News. Retrieved June 3, 2018, from http://www.bbc.co.uk/news/business-25926648
2. Foster, A. (2013, April 10). Add value or die: the fate of corporate information services (Business Information Survey). *Business Information Review*, 30(1).
3. Deloitte. (2018). *2018 Global Human Capital Trends.* London: Deloitte Insights. Retrieved June 3, 2018, from https://www2.deloitte.com/uk/en/pages/human-capital/articles/introduction-human-capital-trends.html
4. The Lawyer. (2017). *UK 200: Workspace Trends 2017.* London: The Lawyer.
5. Carter, D. (2017, August 23). Creativity in action – the information professional is poised to exploit the 4th industrial revolution: The Business Information Survey 2017. *Business Information Review.*
6. Wikiquote. (2018, June 3). Creighton Abrams. Retrieved from Wikiquote: https://simple.wikiquote.org/wiki/Creighton_Abrams
7. Kishore, S. (2013, November). The power of incremental innovation. *Wired.* Retrieved June 3, 2018, from https://www.wired.com/insights/2013/11/the-power-of-incremental-innovation/
8. Brightstarr. (2015, March 15). *Linklater's Award Winning Intranet: Transforming Knowledge Management with SharePoint 2013.* Retrieved June 3, 2018, from Brightstarr: https://www.brightstarr.com/stories/linklaters-enhance-their-knowledge-with-sharepoint-intranet

Further reading

Carter, D. (2017, August 23). Creativity in action – the information professional is poised to exploit the 4th industrial revolution: The Business Information Survey 2017. *Business Information Review.*

Foster, A. (2013, April 10). Add value or die: the fate of corporate information services (Business Information Survey). *Business Information Review*, 30(1).

Goodman, J. (2016). *Robots in Law: How artificial intelligence is transforming legal services*. London: ARK Group.

Kaplan, J. (2015). *Humans Need Not Apply: A guide to wealth & work in the age of artificial intelligence*. Michigan: Yale University Press.

McQuivey, J. (2013). *Digital Disruption: Unleashing the next wave of innovation*. Las Vegas: Amazon Publishing for Forrester Research Inc.

Susskind, R., & Susskind, D. (2015). *The Future of The Professions*. Oxford: Oxford University Press.

UK Commission for Employment and Skills. (2014). *The future of work: jobs and skills in 2030*.

Chapter 9:

Makers in the library – the new age of hands-on artificial intelligence

By Ed Walters, CEO of Fastcase, and Sean Tate, AI sandbox product manager at Fastcase

For decades, computer scientists created software that could take on increasingly difficult discrete tasks, but a generalized artificial intelligence (so-called "strong AI") has proven elusive. Outside of controlled experiments, such as games of chess with carefully-defined rules, artificial intelligence has not yet proven generally useful. However, many computer scientists believe that we are on the cusp of a breakthrough of artificial intelligence, and that this new generation of AI will transform knowledge work every bit as much as the Industrial Revolution transformed industry.

Whether or not we are on the cusp of a revolution of strong AI, it seems clear that software increasingly will perform legal tasks that were previously reserved for lawyers, paralegals, and information professionals. AI may not replace lawyers, but AI will absolutely replace legal work. A great deal of the money paid by clients for those legal services will therefore go to the architects of that software.

Will this be an information oligopoly, with the benefits of AI accruing to a small number of publishers and software companies, at the expense of law firms, law schools, and libraries? Or will the benefits be widespread, like the creation of electric power?

The answer, in part, lies with how broadly the providers of legal services and information participate in artificial intelligence. If information professionals cede the "heavy lifting" work of AI to software companies, they will be unlikely to participate in the gains of the new economy. However, if information professionals themselves use AI tools, conduct their own experiments in supervised learning, and learn how to gain new insights from legal data, there is great potential for a broad-based renaissance in legal services, in which everyone has the opportunity to participate.

Understanding the AI workbench

What kinds of insights could law libraries draw from AI tools? At the simplest end of the spectrum, AI tools can help libraries draw important insights from in-house data. For example, law firms can use tools such as IBM's Watson Developer Cloud to convert documents from images to structured text, build chatbots that understand natural language to triage patron requests, or build search engines that run semantic searches over the firm's KM system.

Libraries can use AI tools to help change the way that law school clinics deliver legal services. For example, the Georgetown University Law Center conducts the Iron Tech Lawyer competition, in which nontechnical law student teams work with clients to create apps for justice using Neota Logic. Expert systems such as Neota Logic or A2J Author may not solve every legal problem, but they can help address simple, recurring legal problems at scale. Indeed, one-to-many software tools may be one of the only scalable ways to address the access-to-justice problem. Information professionals in law schools could be the lynchpin to this kind of development.

Artificial intelligence tools also can offer key insights about the cost of different matters in a law firm, helping firms that want to offer fixed-fee engagements compete more effectively for business. One problem that law firms face is that their client-matter billing data isn't structured enough to understand the distribution of costs for different types of matters.

Sophisticated clients are increasingly demanding that their law firms provide alternative fee arrangements, such as fixed-fee billing. However, without structured data, law firms have faced the impossible task of combing through historical billings to add metadata such as the matter type, stage, lawyer, rate, time, and cost – all to understand how to price future matters. AI tools offer the prospect of extracting insights even from unstructured data. This avoids tedious re-keying or data entry for past matters.

Data mash-ups offer even more interesting possibilities. When firms can compare their own internal billing information with public information such as dockets or public law collections, they can provide quantitative marketing materials to potential clients. Instead of touting the firm's expertise generally, firms can demonstrate that they achieve better results faster, and at lower costs.

Perhaps further in the future law libraries will be combining docket sheet data, judicial opinions and AI tools, such as IBM Watson's Personality Insights, to analyze the actions a particular attorney took to generate a positive or negative outcome from a judge. Extrapolating upon that idea, and with a large enough dataset, a law library may be able to create a tool to anticipate reactions from judges or even opposing counsel, to allow their attorneys to best tailor their approach in court.

The open-endedness of the possibilities is pretty thrilling. Law libraries collect so many different kinds of information that it's hard to say ahead of time what cool insights they can derive with AI tools. Data scientists will tell you that it's often hard to know what insights are even possible until they get their hands dirty with the data sets.

The AI dichotomy: read-only and read/write

These insights aren't guaranteed for everyone who uses AI tools in their library. However, they aren't science fiction, either. The only way to see what kind of insights are possible is to use the tools. Artificial intelligence generally can be amorphous and daunting – but specific tools are more manageable.

For example, the IBM Watson Developer Cloud toolkit can be used by anyone. It includes tools such as natural language processors, tone analyzers, and machine learning tools. These are tools that law librarians can use today, in their own libraries (not in some flying-car future, but now). Libraries don't have to be only consumers of search engines – they can build them for themselves.

Law firms and libraries *should* use commercial, end-to-end products that take advantage of artificial intelligence. If these tools become standard, their insights will become table stakes for law firms delivering sophisticated services. However, those insights won't be unique – using "read-only" AI-enabled software for tasks such as eDiscovery or contract review means that one firm would get the same insight as the next. Nevertheless, these tools will define the new floor for legal services.

It will be the read/write tools that define the ceiling for legal services. Law firms contain great troves of data unique to their practices, their firms, and their lawyers. Using artificial intelligence tools to analyze this data will create differentiated insights – a unique advantage in an otherwise un-differentiated market for legal services.

A great shift is coming, as important as the shakeup from typewriter to PC in the office space. The most successful law firms of the next ten years will be the ones that embrace the new tools of the trade. They will understand the law at a deeper level, see trends in litigation before anyone else, manage themselves more efficiently, give quantitative advice, and provide justice for more people at more competitive costs.

In short, we are on the cusp of a great era of cognitive computing for law – and it won't be just software companies and legal publishers wielding these tools, but law libraries as well. The libraries that embrace this opportunity will be more informed and more important in this new era, an important source of competitive advantage.

www.ingramcontent.com/pod-product-compliance
Ingram Content Group UK Ltd.
Pitfield, Milton Keynes, MK11 3LW, UK
UKHW021848150926
8657IPUK00005B/138

9 781783 583409